Religion in Human Culture

The Christian Tradition

WORLD RELIGIONS CURRICULUM DEVELOPMENT CENTER
MINNEAPOLIS, MINNESOTA

Project Co-Directors: Lee Smith and Wes Bodin
Project Assistants: Joan Voigt and Pat Noyes

Argus Communications
Niles, Illinois 60648

Photo Credits

Cover Photos

Dan V. Crowe   middle, middle right
Mark Link, S.J.   left, right, middle left
Jules Zalon/FREE LANCE PHOTOGRAPHERS
 GUILD   top

Page Photos

VI CYR COLOR PHOTO
  AGENCY
 4 Kenneth R. Cyr/CYR
  COLOR PHOTO AGENCY
 5 Jewel Craig/CYR
  COLOR PHOTO AGENCY
 6 Mike Hayman
 9 SHOSTAL ASSOCIATES

11 Weems Hutto
12/13 Bernard Surtz
16/18 THE BETTMANN ARCHIVE
21 National Library of Turin/
 EDITORIAL PHOTOCOLOR
 ARCHIVES, INC.
24 THE BETTMANN ARCHIVE
27 HISTORICAL PICTURES
 SERVICE, INC.
29 Barbara Van Cleve/
 VAN CLEVE PHOTOGRAPHY
33 ROLOC COLOR SLIDES
35 THE BETTMANN ARCHIVE
36 Dr. H. Karmarz/VAN
 CLEVE PHOTOGRAPHY
41 EDITORIAL PHOTOCOLOR
 ARCHIVES, INC.
42 Mark Link, S.J.

44 Dan V. Crowe
48 Mark Link, S.J.
53 ROLOC COLOR SLIDES
56/62 Mark Link, S.J.
69 ROLOC COLOR SLIDES
72 Follett Publishing Co./
 KONRAN MEDIA
74 Erich Hartmann/MAGNUM
 PHOTOS, INC.
77 Charles Harbutt/MAGNUM
 PHOTOS, INC.
80 Mark Link, S.J.
82 Algimantas Kezys, S.J.
85 Mark Link, S.J.
89 ROLOC COLOR SLIDES
90 John J. Cumming
93 Mark Link, S.J.
96 THE BETTMANN ARCHIVE

104/109 John J. Cumming
110 THE BETTMANN ARCHIVE
119 Jean-Claude Lejeune
122/125 HISTORICAL PICTURES
 SERVICE, INC.
127 Dan V. Crowe
130/131/134 Follett Publishing Co./
 KONRAN MEDIA
141 Dan V. Crowe
144 THE BETTMANN ARCHIVE
147/152/158 HISTORICAL PICTURES
 SERVICE, INC.
160 Copyright, 1889, THE LOS
 ANGELES TIMES.
 Reprinted by permission.
165 Bruce Anspach/EDITORIAL
 PHOTOCOLOR ARCHIVES,
 INC.

Acknowledgments

Lyrics for "Amazing Grace" from the *Baptist Standard Hymnal.* Copyright 1973 by the Sunday School Publishing Board, National Baptist Convention, U.S.A. Reprinted by permission.

Excerpt from *Documents of the Christian Church,* 2d ed., edited by Henry Bettenson. Copyright © 1963 by Oxford University Press. Reprinted by permission of Oxford University Press, Oxford.

"A Medieval Diocese" and "The Orders of Society" as quoted in Robert Boutruche, *Seigneurie et Feodalite,* copyright 1959 by Aubier, Paris. Translated by John M. Good in *The Shaping of Western Society,* copyright © 1968 by Holt, Rinehart and Winston, Inc. Reprinted by permission of Georges Borchardt, Inc., and Holt, Rinehart and Winston.

Excerpt from *A Handbook of Theological Terms* by Van A. Harvey. Copyright © Van A. Harvey 1964. Reprinted (with slight changes) with permission of Macmillan Publishing Co., Inc.

Excerpts from *Europe in the Middle Ages,* Second Edition, by Robert S. Hoyt, © 1957, 1966, by Harcourt Brace Jovanovich, Inc., and reprinted with their permission.

Excerpts from *Readings in Western Civilization* by Paul L. Hughes and Robert F. Fries. Copyright 1956 by Littlefield, Adams & Co. Reprinted by permission of the publisher.

Excerpt from *Yearbook of American and Canadian Churches 1977,* edited by Constant H. Jacquet, Jr. Copyright © 1977 by the National Council of the Churches of Christ in the United States of America. Reprinted by permission.

Excerpt from *Medieval Political Ideas,* Vol. 2, by Ewart Lewis. Copyright 1954 by Alfred A. Knopf, Inc. Reprinted by permission of Alfred A. Knopf, Inc.

Excerpt from *Handbook of Denominations in the United States,* new 6th ed., by Frank S. Mead. Copyright © 1975 by Abingdon Press. Reprinted by permission.

The texts of the Apostles' Creed, the Nicene Creed, and the Lord's Prayer taken from *Prayers We Have in Common* are those prepared by the International Consultation on English Texts, 1975, and are used by permission.

The United States portion of the map "Ranking Christian Denominations in the United States and Canada" is based on a map published by the Glenmary Research Center, Washington, D.C. Copyright © 1974 by the National Council of Churches of Christ in the U.S.A. Reprinted with permission.

Excerpts from *The Revised Standard Version Common Bible.* Copyright © 1973 by the Division of Christian Education of the National Council of the Churches of Christ in the United States of America. Reprinted by permission.

Excerpt from *A New Eusebius* edited by J. Stevenson. Copyright © 1957 by J. Stevenson. Reprinted by permission of The Society for Promoting Christian Knowledge, London.

Excerpt from *Civilization Past and Present,* Vol. 1, Third Edition, by T. Walter Wallbank and Alastair M. Taylor. Copyright 1954 by Scott, Foresman and Company. Reprinted by permission.

Lyrics from *He Lived the Good Life* by Richard Wilson. Copyright © 1973 by Wil-Song, Inc. Reprinted by permission. *He Lived the Good Life* is available in record album, 8 track tape, and songbook form through Wil-Song, Inc., and Augsburg Publishing, Minneapolis, Minnesota.

Religion in Human Culture is a project of St. Louis Park Independent School District #283, Title III/IV (Part C), ESEA, and the Northwest Area Foundation. The opinions and other contents of this book do not necessarily reflect the position or policy of the State of Minnesota, the U.S. Government, St. Louis Park ISD #283, or the Northwest Area Foundation, and no official endorsement should be inferred.

Every effort has been made to trace the owners of copyright material in this book. Should any material have been included inadvertently without the permission of the copyright owner, acknowledgment will be made in any future edition.

Design by Gene Tarpey
Maps by Homer Grooman and
Hillard Chamerlik

Argus Communications
7440 Natchez Avenue
Niles, Illinois 60648

International Standard Book Number:
0-89505-013-7

Library of Congress Number:
78-53804

0 9 8 7 6 5 4 3 2

Contents

Note to the Reader

This book is a collection of readings which have been taken from a variety of sources. It is not to be considered or used as a conventional textbook; rather, the readings are intended as a source of data or information on various practices and concepts found in the Christian tradition. A study and analysis of this data should increase your understanding not only of Christianity but of the people who practice this tradition.

To facilitate your reading a glossary of several terms relevant to Christianity is provided at the back of this book. As you encounter words you are unfamiliar with, refer to the glossary for their definitions.

A New England Baptist church.

READING 1

Religious Denominations in the United States and Canada

A. United States*

Adventists
   Seventh-day Adventists
   Advent Christian Church
   Church of God (General Conference)
   Primitive Advent Christian Church
African Orthodox Church
Amana Church Society
American Ethical Union
American Evangelical Christian Churches
American Ministerial Association
American Rescue Workers
Anglican Orthodox Church
Apostolic Christian Church (Nazarean)
Apostolic Christian Church of America
Apostolic Faith
Apostolic Overcoming Holy Church of God
Armenian Churches
Assemblies of God (General Council of)
Baha'i
Baptists
   American Baptist Churches in the U.S.A.
   Southern Baptist Convention

*From the Table of Contents in Frank S. Mead, *Handbook of Denominations in the United States,* new 6th ed. (Nashville, Tenn.: Abingdon Press, 1975).

Negro Baptists
American Baptist Association
Baptist Bible Fellowship, International
Baptist General Conference
Baptist Missionary Association of America
Bethel Ministerial Association
Central Baptist Association
Christian Unity Baptist Association
Conservative Baptist Association of America
Duck River (and Kindred) Associations of
    Baptists (Baptist Church of Christ)
Free Will Baptists
General Baptists
General Association of Regular Baptist Churches
General Conference of the Evangelical Baptist Church, Inc.
General Six-Principle Baptists
Landmark Baptists
National Baptist Evangelical Life and Soul
    Saving Assembly of the U.S.A.
National Primitive Baptist Convention of the U.S.A.
North American Baptist General Conference
Primitive Baptists
Separate Baptists in Christ
Seventh Day Baptists
Seventh Day Baptists (German, 1728)
Two-Seed-in-the-Spirit Predestinarian Baptists
United Baptists
United Free Will Baptist Church

Bible Fellowship Church
Bible Protestant Church
Bible Way Church, World Wide
Black Muslims
Brethren (Dunkers)
  Church of the Brethren
  Brethren Church (National Fellowship of
    Brethren Churches)
  Old German Baptist Brethren (Old Order Dunkers)

Plymouth Brethren
River Brethren
  Brethren in Christ

Old Order, or Yorker, Brethren
United Zion Church
United Brethren
    Church of the United Brethren in Christ
    United Christian Church

Buddhism
Christadelphians
Christian and Missionary Alliance
Christian Catholic Church
Christian Church of North America
Christian Church (Disciples of Christ)
Christian Churches and Churches of Christ
Christian Congregation
Christian Nation Church U.S.A.
Christian Union
Christ's Sanctified Holy Church
Church of Christ (Holiness) U.S.A.
Church of Christ, Scientist
Church of God
    Church of God (Apostolic)
    The (Original) Church of God, Inc.
    Church of God (Anderson, Indiana)
    Church of God (Seventh Day)
    Church of God and Saints in Christ
    Church of God by Faith, Inc.
    Church of God in Christ
    Church of God in Christ (International)
    Worldwide Church of God

Church of Illumination
Church of Jesus Christ of Latter-day Saints (Mormons)
    Church of Jesus Christ of Latter-day Saints
    Reorganized Church of Jesus Christ of Latter-day Saints
    Church of Christ (Temple Lot)
    Church of Jesus Christ
    Church of Jesus Christ of Latter-day Saints (Strangites)

Church of Our Lord Jesus Christ of the Apostolic Faith, Inc.
Church of the Nazarene
Churches of Christ
Churches of Christ in Christian Union
Churches of God, Holiness

Churches of God in North America (General Eldership)
Churches of the Living God
Churches of the New Jerusalem
Congregational Christian Churches (National Association)
Congregational Holiness Church
Conservative Congregational Christian Conference
Divine Science
Eastern Churches
   Albanian Orthodox Archdiocese in America
   American Carpatho-Russian Orthodox Greek Catholic Church
   American Holy Orthodox Catholic Apostolic Eastern Church
   Antiochian Churches
   Bulgarian Eastern Orthodox Church
   Eastern Orthodox Catholic Church in America
   Greek Archdiocese of North and South America
   Holy Apostolic and Catholic Church of the East (Assyrians)
   Holy Orthodox Church in America (Eastern Catholic
     and Apostolic)
   Romanian Orthodox Episcopate of America
   Russian Orthodox Church
   Serbian Orthodox Church in the U.S.A. and Canada
   Ukranian Orthodox Churches
Episcopal Church
   Reformed Episcopal Church
Evangelical Church of North America
Evangelical Congregational Church
Evangelical Covenant Church of America
Evangelical Free Church of America
Federated Churches
Fire Baptized Holiness Church
Fire Baptized Holiness Church (Wesleyan)
Free Christian Zion Church of Christ
Friends
   Friends General Conference
   Friends United Meeting (Five Years Meeting)
   Religious Society of Friends (Conservative)
House of David
Independent Assemblies of God International
Independent Churches
Independent Fundamental Churches of America
International Church of the Foursquare Gospel

An Advent Christian Church, Connecticut.

A Church of Christ, Scientist, Connecticut.

Jehovah's Witnesses
Jewish Congregations
   Orthodox Judaism
   Reform Judaism
   Conservative Judaism
   Black Jews
Kodesh Church of Immanuel
Liberal Catholic Church
Light of the Way Open Door Church
     Fellowship, International
Lutherans
   American Lutheran Church
   Lutheran Church in America
   Church of the Lutheran Brethren of America
   Evangelical Lutheran Synod
   Apostolic Lutheran Church of America
   The Lutheran Church—Missouri Synod
   Protestant Conference (Lutheran)
   Wisconsin Evangelical Lutheran Synod
Mennonites
   Beachy Amish Mennonite Church
   Church of God in Christ (Mennonite)
   Conservative Mennonite Conference
   Evangelical Mennonite Brethren
   Evangelical Mennonite Church
   General Conference Mennonite Church
   Hutterian Brethren
   Mennonite Brethren Church of North America
   Mennonite Church
   Old Order Amish Mennonite Church
   Old Order (Wisler) Mennonite Church
   Reformed Mennonite Church
   Unaffiliated Mennonites
Methodists
   The United Methodist Church
   African Methodist Episcopal Church
   African Methodist Episcopal Zion Church
   African Union First Colored Methodist Protestant Church, Inc.
   Christian Methodist Episcopal Church
   Congregational Methodist Church
   First Congregational Methodist Church of the U.S.A.

   Cumberland Methodist Church
   Evangelical Methodist Church
   Free Methodist Church of North America
   Fundamental Methodist Church, Inc.
   Independent African Methodist Episcopal Church
   New Congregational Methodist Church
   People's Methodist Church
   Primitive Methodist Church, U.S.A.
   Reformed Methodist Union Episcopal Church
   Reformed Zion Union Apostolic Church
   Southern Methodist Church
   Union American Methodist Episcopal Church
Metropolitan Church Association
Missionary Church
Moravians
   Moravian Church (Unitas Fratrum)
   Unity of the Brethren
Muslims
National David Spiritual Temple of Christ Church Union (Inc.), U.S.A.
New Apostolic Church of North America
Old Catholic Churches
   American Catholic Church, Archdiocese of New York
   American Catholic Church (Syro-Antiochian)
   North American Old Roman Catholic Church
   Old Roman Catholic Church in Europe and America
     (English Rite)
Open Bible Standard Churches, Inc.
Pentecostal Bodies
   Calvary Pentecostal Church, Inc.
   Elim Fellowship
   Emmanuel Holiness Church
   International Pentecostal Assemblies
   Pentecostal Assemblies of the World, Inc.
   Pentecostal Church of Christ
   Pentecostal Church of God of America, Inc.
   Pentecostal Fire-Baptized Holiness Church
   Pentecostal Free-Will Baptist Church, Inc.
   Pentecostal Holiness Church
   United Pentecostal Church International
Pillar of Fire
Polish National Catholic Church of America

A Latino Pentecostal church in the Midwest.

Presbyterians
    United Presbyterian Church in the U.S.A.
    Presbyterian Church in the U.S.
    Associate Presbyterian Church of North America
    Associate Reformed Presbyterian Church
    Bible Presbyterian Church
    Cumberland Presbyterian Church
    Second Cumberland Presbyterian Church in the U.S.
    Orthodox Presbyterian Church
    Reformed Presbyterian Church, Evangelical Synod
    Reformed Presbyterian Church of North America

Reformed Bodies
    Reformed Church in America
    Christian Reformed Church
    Hungarian Reformed Church in America
    Netherlands Reformed Congregations
    Protestant Reformed Churches of America
    Reformed Church in the United States

Roman Catholic Church
Salvation Army
Schwenkfelder Church
Social Brethren
Spiritualists
    International General Assembly of Spiritualists
    National Spiritualist Alliance of the U.S.A.
    National Spiritualist Association of Churches
    Progressive Spiritual Church

Theosophy
Triumph the Church and Kingdom of God in Christ
Unitarian Universalist Association
United Church of Christ
    Congregational Church
    Christian Church
    Evangelical and Reformed Church
    United Church of Christ

United Holy Church of America, Inc.
Unity School of Christianity
Vedanta Society
Volunteers of America
Wesleyan Church

B. Canada*

The Anglican Church of Canada
The Antiochian Orthodox Christian,
   Archdiocese of North America
Apostolic Christian Church (Nazarean)
Apostolic Church of Pentecost of Canada
Armenian Church of North America, Diocese of Canada
Associated Gospel Churches
Baptist Federation of Canada
Baptist General Conference
Bible Holiness Movement
Brethren in Christ Church, Canadian Conference
Buddhist Church in Canada
Canadian Baptist Conference
Canadian Jewish Congress
Canadian Yearly Meeting of the Religious Society of Friends
The Christian and Missionary Alliance in Canada
Christian Church (Disciples of Christ)
Christian Churches and Churches of Christ in Canada
Christian Community & Brotherhood
   of Reformed Doukhobors
The Christian Congregation
Church of God (Anderson, Ind.)
Church of God (Cleveland, Tenn.)
The Church of God of Prophecy in Canada
The Church of Jesus Christ of Latter-day Saints in Canada
Church of the Lutheran Brethren of America
Church of the Nazarene
Conference of Mennonites in Canada of the General Conference
   Mennonite Church
Evangelical Baptist Churches in Canada, the Fellowship of
The Evangelical Church in Canada
The Evangelical Covenant Church of Canada
The Evangelical Lutheran Church of Canada
Evangelical Mennonite Conference
Evangelical Mennonite Mission Conference
Free Methodist Church in Canada
Greek Orthodox Archdiocese of N. & S. America,
   Ninth Archdiocesan District

*From Constant H. Jacquet, Jr., ed., *Yearbook of American and Canadian Churches 1977*
   (Nashville, Tenn.: Abingdon Press, 1977), pp. 241–43.

A United Church of Canada, Nova Scotia.

Independent Assemblies of God—Canada
Independent Holiness Church
International Church of the Foursquare Gospel—
    Western Canada District
The Italian Pentecostal Church of Canada
Jehovah's Witnesses
Lutheran Church—Canada
Lutheran Church in America—Canada Section
Mennonite Brethren Churches of North America,
    Canadian Conference of the
Mennonite Church (Canada)
The Missionary Church—Canada
Moravian Church in America—Northern Province,
    Canadian District of the
North American Baptist Conference
The Old Catholic Church of Canada
The Pentecostal Assemblies of Canada
Pentecostal Assemblies of Newfoundland
Polish National Catholic Church of Canada
The Presbyterian Church in Canada
Primitive Baptist Convention of New Brunswick
Reformed Church in America—Ontario Classis
Reformed Presbyterian Church, Evangelical Synod
Reorganized Church of Jesus Christ of Latter-day Saints
The Roman Catholic Church in Canada
The Romanian Orthodox Church in America (Canadian Parishes)
The Romanian Orthodox Episcopate of America (Jackson, Mich.)
Russian Orthodox Church in Canada Patriarchal Parishes
Seventh-Day Adventist Church in Canada
Ukrainian Greek Catholic Church in Canada
Union of Spiritual Communities of Christ
    (Orthodox Doukhobors in Canada)
Unitarian Universalist Association
United Brethren in Christ, Ontario Conference
United Church of Canada
The Wesleyan Church
Wisconsin Evangelical Lutheran Synod

READING 2

What It Means to Be a Christian

The following statements are representative of several hundred responses given by high school students in reply to the question, "What does it mean to be a Christian?"

- To be holy.
- A Christian is someone who believes Christ exists. Christians can worship Christ in different ways.
- Being a Christian to me means that I have accepted Christ into my life. It is an intrapersonal relationship with Jesus Christ.
- Belief in Christ and God—one God. Belief that He is the creator of the universe, that He guides what we do and what happens on earth and throughout the universe. Belief that He is good.
- To trust Christ with all aspects of your life.
- I feel being a Christian is to be as much like Christ as possible, to follow Christ's commandments—just to do what Christ would want you to do, or as Christ would do.
- To believe in and follow the teachings of Christ and not of the world.
- It means that you believe in Christ and will obey the laws according to the Bible, and that you have been baptized, which is total immersion for remission of your sins, and are filled with the Holy Spirit.
- Being a Christian means following the teachings of Christ whatever hardships you might encounter.

Singing a solo at a Baptist church service.

- To follow the word of God by using the guidelines of the Bible and by showing the love He gave you.
- To believe in the Apostles' Creed and to carry out good works according to Jesus' life.
- To believe in Jesus Christ and serving to spread love, understanding, and the word of God to people regardless of nationality, color, or belief.
- To set your values in accordance with God and the Bible (not all values though).
- To be a Christian is to believe in Jesus Christ and His teachings and to act upon them toward other people, and to spread the word.
- Christianity is believing that Jesus Christ is the son of God and that He died to take away your sins, and only by faith can you receive salvation.
- It means you have accepted Christ as your personal Savior and Lord, and you have completely given your life to Him.
- It means to be wholly dedicated to do the Lord's will and to block out the devil's ways of thinking.
- It means to live a good life, to believe in one God, and to make the most out of what you have.
- To go by the Ten Commandments.
- It means caring for others more than you care for yourself.
- *To me,* being a Christian is being sensitive to what exists within others (i.e., thoughts, emotions, etc.) and reacting to them and caring about them as your own.
- To believe in God's forgiving grace and love Him.
- It means to believe in God our father, His son, Jesus Christ, who died for us, and the Holy Spirit who makes us one. Follow the teachings of Christ.
- Love, fear, and believe in God.
- It means I rely on God instead of myself to help me through my problems.
- To believe in one divine God, creator of all heaven and earth, who conceived a son through the Virgin Mary, to save our souls and open the gates of heaven.
- To have complete faith and belief in God.
- To know that the Lord will come back and take you with Him and He will help you in troubled times.
- To know that you will have eternal life when being born again through Christ.

Baptist churchgoers in silent devotion.

A Baptist choir sings during part of a Sunday service.

- To ask God into your heart to be your everlasting Savior, and to be able to pray to Him and get answers to your prayers.
- It gives me the right to enter the pearly gates of heaven and see my Maker; it uplifts my soul when I am depressed; it gives me hope and faith and something to believe in; it gives me moral guides in which to lead a holy life so I am able to attain eternal life.
- A person who goes to church.
- It means to follow the Bible twenty-four hours a day, to not be hypocritical, also to follow everything (all the laws) set out in the Bible, not just the ones you like.
- To be a Christian is to know that I am alive and living—held together by a spiritual force of nature mentally and physically.
- To respect and follow the ideas of Christianity. To believe in yourself, learn how to help yourself and others, and learn how to adapt to problems which must be solved in life through interpreting the values and ideas of Christianity.
- To stand up for your feelings for God and to make good of your life, and if you should sin, to confess your sins.
- To fulfill the requirements of your church or faith.
- Believing in Christ and following His teachings, and maybe someday meeting your Creator.
- To believe in God any way you want. Not going to church doesn't mean you aren't religious.
- A Christian is someone who believes in the teachings of God and follows those teachings. I don't think people can consider themselves Christians if they would rather "sleep in on Sunday."
- It means believing in Jesus Christ, accepting Him as your Savior, receiving the Holy Spirit and, eventually, eternal life.

READING 3

Creeds

WES BODIN AND LEE SMITH

In order to gain an understanding of Christianity, we will begin by examining the creeds of the church. First we will consider what creeds are, how they have developed over the years, and how the churches use creeds. Then in Readings 4 and 5, we will examine the content of the creeds themselves.

The word *creed* comes from the Latin word *credo,* which means "I believe." A creed is a summary of what is believed, or held, in faith. Because a creed is a believer's statement of what is believed, it is known essentially by "insiders" just as the Pledge of Allegiance is more apt to be known by Americans than "outsiders." In a sense, creeds are symbols; that is, they carry concepts which are greater than the language itself. Some Christians call these concepts "mysteries of faith." These mysteries are events, actions, and processes which may be classified as supernatural because they cannot be explained in logical or scientific ways. Accepting the logical and the scientific requires explanation and understanding. Accepting that which is a mystery is an act of faith; and in the final analysis, Christianity is a faith religion.

Many statements in the Bible might be considered creedal in nature because they declare what is believed. In the Jewish tradition the Shema—"Hear, O Israel: The Lord our God, the Lord is one" (Deuteronomy 6:4)—has historically served as a Jewish affirmation of monotheism. Saint Peter's response to Jesus—

"You are the Christ, the Son of the Living God" (Matthew 16:16)—and Saint Paul's statement—"Jesus Christ is Lord" (Philippians 2:11)—are both creedal assertions of what Christians believe.

The development of creeds in the Christian community became well established in the early years of the church. They began as relatively simple statements and became more complex through time. The first creeds were baptismal creeds, or statements, in which the candidate for baptism declared his or her faith. The pattern of these early creeds was always Trinitarian in nature. They were, no doubt, a response to the "great commission" of Christ: "Go, therefore, and make disciples of all nations, baptizing them in the name of the Father, and of the Son, and of the Holy Spirit" (Matthew 28:19). The Apostles' Creed, which has no known author, seems to be the most enduring of the early creeds. It reaches from the early days of the Christians to the present.

In the first century the number of Christians was small, and communication problems were relatively simple. As Christianity expanded to more remote places, variations in the meaning of faith and practice began to develop. Over time these variations threatened to break the unity of the church. Growing disagreement about the human and divine nature of Christ led the Roman emperor Constantine to call a council of bishops, or church leaders, at Nicaea in 325 A.D. Some have argued that Constantine's motives were political, rather than religious; however, the results of the council were to have a lasting imprint on Christian teaching. The major accomplishment of the council was the development of the Nicene Creed, which more clearly defined what Christians believed about God, his work, and the Holy Trinity. This creed most emphatically stated that Jesus Christ was truly God ("the only Son of God, eternally begotten of the Father, God from God, Light from Light, true Son from true God, begotten, not made, one in Being with the Father"). It also made clear that Jesus was truly man ("For us men and for our salvation he came down from heaven: by the power of the Holy Spirit he was born of the Virgin Mary, and became man").

The profile of Emperor Constantine on a gold Roman coin from A.D. 339.

Creeds have been used by Christians in at least four ways.

1. Creeds have been used as a baptismal commitment, or promise, of what an individual believes. The classical, or traditional, baptismal declaration is the Apostles' Creed.

2. Creeds have been used to clarify the basic teachings of Christianity. The Nicene Creed is an example. This process of clarification has continued through the ages, and other specialized statements have been developed.

3. Creeds have served as the core for the instructional programs and teaching ministries of many churches.

4. Creeds have played an important part in the liturgy, or public worship, of many churches (Eastern Orthodox, Roman Catholic, Episcopal, Lutheran, Reformed, Presbyterian, Methodist, and others). In worship, the creed is a pledge of allegiance, a summarizing declaration of belief, and, particularly, a response to the Word of God proclaimed in the Bible. Typically, the Nicene Creed has been associated with the Eucharist, or Holy Communion, and the Apostles' Creed with Holy Baptism. It should be noted that the same creeds are sometimes stated individually, "I believe . . . ," emphasizing individual commitment. In other instances the creed may be stated collectively, "We believe . . . ," emphasizing the community or shared quality of belief.

The Apostles' Creed and the Nicene Creed are universally accepted by most Christians. Even those Christians who reject the liturgical use of creeds in their worship generally accept the content of the creeds. The Apostles' and the Nicene creeds are often referred to as the ecumenical, or catholic, creeds. Catholic, in this case, does not refer to the Roman Catholic church but rather the universal quality of the church, that is, the idea that the church is open to all human beings regardless of race, sex, wealth, or ethnic heritage. The word *catholic* is derived from the Greek words *kata* ("concerning") and *holos* ("the whole").

Because of its universal acceptance we shall now focus on the Nicene Creed as a basis for understanding what Christians, in general, believe. Two translations of the Nicene Creed (Reading 4) and of the Apostles' Creed (Reading 5) are provided to deepen your understanding.

The Council of Nicaea (A.D. 325).

READING 4

The Nicene Creed

The following version of the Nicene Creed is taken from The Book of Common Prayer.*

I believe in one God the Father Almighty, Maker of heaven and earth, And of all things visible and invisible:

And in one Lord Jesus Christ, the only-begotten Son of God; Begotten of his Father before all worlds, God of God, Light of Light, Very God of very God; Begotten, not made; Being of one substance with the Father; By whom all things were made: Who for us men and for our salvation came down from heaven, And was incarnate by the Holy Ghost of the Virgin Mary, And was made man: And was crucified also for us under Pontius Pilate; He suffered and was buried: And the third day he rose again according to the Scriptures: And ascended into heaven, And sitteth on the right hand of the Father: And he shall come again, with glory, to judge both the quick and the dead; Whose kingdom shall have no end.

And I believe in the Holy Ghost, The Lord, and Giver of Life, Who proceedeth from the Father and the Son; Who with the Father and the Son together is worshipped and glorified; Who spake by the Prophets: And I believe one Catholic and Apostolic

*From *The Book of Common Prayer,* According to the Use of the Episcopal Church in the United States of America (New York: The Church Hymnal Corporation, 1928), p. 71.

Church: I acknowledge one Baptism for the remission of sins: And I look for the Resurrection of the dead: And the Life of the world to come. Amen.

The following version is from Prayers We Have in Common.*

We believe in one God,
    the Father, the Almighty,
    maker of heaven and earth,
    of all that is, seen and unseen.

We believe in one Lord, Jesus Christ,
    the only Son of God,
    eternally begotten of the Father,
    God from God, Light from Light,
    true God from true God,
    begotten, not made,
    of one Being with the Father.
    Through him all things were made.
For us men and for our salvation
    he came down from heaven:
by the power of the Holy Spirit
    he became incarnate from the Virgin Mary, and was made man.
For our sake he was crucified under Pontius Pilate;
    he suffered death and was buried.
    On the third day he rose again
      in accordance with the Scriptures;
    he ascended into heaven
      and is seated at the right hand of the Father.
He will come again in glory to judge the living and the dead,
    and his kingdom will have no end.

We believe in the Holy Spirit, the Lord, the giver of life,
    who proceeds from the Father [and the Son].
    With the Father and the Son he is worshiped and glorified.
    He has spoken through the Prophets.
    We believe in one holy catholic and apostolic Church.
    We acknowledge one baptism for the forgiveness of sins.
    We look for the resurrection of the dead,
      and the life of the world to come. Amen.

*From International Consultation on English Texts, *Prayers We Have in Common,* 2d rev. ed. (Philadelphia: Fortress Press, 1975), p. 6.

READING 6
Some Demographics on Christianity

	U.S.A.	Canada	World	Creed Based	Liturgical Worship	Polity[1]
		(in millions)				
1. Roman Catholic	48.9	9.4	540.7	Yes	Yes	E
2. Baptist	25.8	.2	29.0	No	No	C
3. Methodist	12.8	*	18.0	No	No	M
4. Lutheran	8.6	.3	75.0	Yes	Yes	M
5. Eastern Orthodox	4.2	.3	86.6	Yes	Yes	E
6. Presbyterian	3.8	.2	Included in Reformed Churches	Yes	No	P
7. Episcopal (Anglican)	2.9	1.0	45.0	Yes	Yes	E
8. Latter-day Saints (Mormons)	2.5	.1	3.0	No	No	O
9. United Church of Canada	—	2.1	2.1	No	No	C
10. United Church of Christ	1.8	—	1.8	No	No	C
11. Christian Church (Disciples of Christ)	1.3	*	1.4	No	No	C
12. Assemblies of God	1.2	*	1.4	No	No	M
13. Christian Churches and Churches of Christ	1.0	*	1.0	No	No	C
14. Reformed Churches	.7	*	35.2	Yes	No	P

*Fewer than 100,000 members

[1]Polity, or pattern of church government (generalized):
C—congregational   E—episcopal   O—other
P—presbyterian   M—mixed

The above 14 major groups of Christians constitute 92 percent of the 140 million Christians in the United States and Canada. The other 8 percent are found in about 250 diverse groups, most of which have fewer than 500,000 members.

Data are based on the following sources:
Constant H. Jacquet, Jr., ed., *Yearbook of American and Canadian Churches, 1977* (Nashville, Tenn.: Abingdon Press, 1977).
Encyclopaedia Britannica, 15th ed. (1975).

A nineteenth-century lithograph shows a Christian martyr being led into the Roman Colosseum.

READING 7

The Martyrs of Lyons and Vienne, 177*

The servants of Christ who sojourn at Vienne and Lyons in Gaul to the brethren in Asia and Phrygia who have the same faith and hope as we of redemption: peace and grace and glory from God the Father, and Christ Jesus our Lord.

. . . Indeed we are unable, and it is beyond the power of pen, to state with exactitude the greatness of the affliction here, the mighty rage of the heathen against the saints, and all that the blessed martyrs endured. For the adversary fell upon us with all his might, and gave us already a foretaste of what his coming in the future without restraint would be. He left nothing undone to train and exercise beforehand his own against the servants of God, insomuch that not only were we excluded from houses and baths and market-place, but they even forbade any of us to be seen at all in any place whatsoever. Nevertheless the grace of God was our captain on the other side, rescued the weak, and ranged against the foe firm pillars, able by their endurance to draw upon themselves the whole attack of the evil one. And these joined battle, enduring every kind of reproach and punishment. Yea, regarding their many trials as little, they hastened to Christ, truly showing that the sufferings of this present time are not worthy to be compared with the glory which shall be revealed to us-ward.

*Slightly adapted from J. Stevenson, ed., *A New Eusebius* (London: S.P.C.K., 1957), pp. 31–40.

First of all they nobly endured the attacks which the whole mass of the people heaped upon them, clamours, blows, halings, plunderings, stonings and confinements, and all that an infuriated mob is wont to employ against foes and enemies. Then they were conducted to the market-place by the tribune and the authorities presiding over the city. And when they had been questioned before the whole multitude, and given their testimony, they were shut up in prison until the governor's arrival. But afterwards, when they were brought before the governor, who used all the usual savagery against us, Vettius Epagathus, one of the brethren, a man filled with the fulness of love toward God and his neighbour, came forward. His conduct had reached such a degree of perfection that, young though he was, his reputation equalled that of the elder Zacharias; for he had walked in all the commandments and ordinances of the Lord blameless. In every service to his neighbour he was untiring, having a great zeal for God and fervent in spirit. Such a man could not endure the passing of so groundless a judgement against us; but was exceeding angry, and requested that he himself might be heard in defence of the brethren, that there is nothing godless or impious among us. Those around the tribunal cried out against him (for he was indeed a man of note), and the governor would not listen to the just request he had thus put forward, but asked him this one question, if he too were a Christian. And having confessed in a very clear voice, he also attained to the inheritance of the martyrs, being called the advocate of Christians, but having the Advocate in himself, the Spirit of Zacharias; which Spirit he showed in the fulness of his love, in that he was well pleased to lay down even his own life for the defence of the brethren. For he was and is a true disciple of Christ, following the Lamb whithersoever he goeth.

Henceforward the rest were divided. Some were manifestly ready for martyrdom, and fulfilled with all zeal the confession wherein they gave witness, but others were manifestly unready and untrained and still weak, unable to bear the strain of a mighty conflict: of which number some ten proved abortions. These last wrought in us great sorrow and immeasurable mourning, and hindered the zeal of the remainder who had not yet been seized, and who in spite of every terrible suffering nevertheless attended the martyrs and would not leave them. But then we were all greatly affrighted at the uncertainty of confession; not that we feared the punishments inflicted, but we looked to the issue and dreaded lest any should fall away. Nevertheless those who were worthy were seized day by day, thus filling up the number of the former class, so that from the two churches were gathered all the zealous members, by whose means our position here had been mainly established. And there were seized also certain of our heathen household servants, since the governor gave an official order that we should all be sought out. And they too, thanks to the snares of Satan, in their fear of the tortures which they saw the saints enduring, and at the instigation of the soldiers, falsely accused us of Thyestean banquets[1] and Oedipean intercourse,[2] and things of which it is not right for us to speak or think, nay, not even to believe that the like was ever done by man. But these rumours spread, and all were infuriated at us, insomuch that those who had formerly acted with moderation, on the ground of friendship, were now greatly incensed and cut to the heart against us. Thus was fulfilled that which was said by the Lord: The time will come, when whosoever killeth you shall think that he offereth service unto God. From that time on the holy martyrs endured punishments beyond all description, Satan earnestly endeavouring to elicit from their lips also some of the slanders.

But the entire fury of the crowd, governor and soldiers fell upon Sanctus, the deacon from Vienne, and upon Maturus, a noble combatant though but lately baptized, and upon Attalus, a native of Pergamum, of which church he had been always the pillar and ground, and upon Blandina, through whom Christ showed that things which appear mean and unsightly and despicable in the eyes of men are accounted worthy of great glory in the sight of God, through love towards Him, a love which showed itself in power and did not boast itself in appearance. For when we were all afraid, and her mistress according to the flesh (who was herself also a combatant in the ranks of the martyrs) was in a state of agony, lest the weakness of her body should render her unable to make a bold confession, Blandina was filled with such power that those who by turns kept torturing her in every way from dawn till evening were worn out and exhausted, and themselves confessed defeat from lack of aught else to do to her. They marvelled that the breath still remained in a body all mangled and covered with gaping wounds, and they testified that a single form of torture was sufficient to render life extinct, let alone such and so many. But

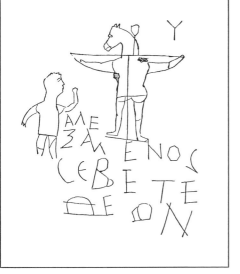

A Heathen caricature of Christ from A.D. 200, drawn on a wall of a Roman palace. The Greek inscription says, "Alexamenus worshipping his God."

[1]Eating of human flesh.
[2]Intercourse with parent of opposite sex.

the blessed woman, like a noble champion, in confession regained her strength. And for her, to say "I am a Christian, and with us no evil finds a place" was refreshment and rest and insensibility to her lot.

Now as for Sanctus, he also nobly endured with surpassing and superhuman courage all the torments that human hands could inflict. And though the wicked men hoped that the continuance and severity of the tortures would cause him to utter something that he ought not, he set the battle against them with such firmness that he would not state even his own name, or the people or city whence he came, or whether he were bond or free. But to every question he replied in Latin: "I am a Christian." This he confessed again and again, instead of name and city and race and all else, and no other word did the heathen hear from his lips. Hence there actually arose great contention on the part of the governor and the torturers against him, with the result that finally, when nothing else was left to inflict upon him, they applied red-hot brazen plates to the most tender parts of his body. And though these were burning, Sanctus himself remained unbending and unyielding, and firm in his confession; for he was bedewed and strengthened by the heavenly fountain of the water of life which issues from the bowels of Christ. But his poor body was a witness to what he had undergone—one whole wound and bruise, contracted, having lost the outward form of a man—in which body Christ suffered and accomplished mighty wonders, bringing the adversary to nought and showing for the example of those that remained that nothing is to be feared where the love of the Father is, nothing is painful where there is the glory of Christ. For the wicked men after certain days again tortured the martyr, thinking to overcome him when they applied the same instruments to limbs so swollen and enflamed that he could not bear even the hand to touch them; or that he would rather die under the tortures and so cause terror to the rest. Yet not only did nothing of the kind occur in this case, but, contrary to all human expectation, the poor body actually arose and became erect under the subsequent tortures, and regained its former shape and the use of its limbs. Thus by the grace of Christ the second torturing proved for him not punishment but healing. And Biblis too, one of those who had denied, the devil supposed that he had already devoured. But wishing to use her slander as a further ground of condemnation, he brought her to punishment, that he might compel an already fragile and craven woman to state impieties concerning us. She, however, regained her senses under the torture and awoke, so to speak, out of a deep sleep, when the passing retribution recalled to her mind the eternal punishment in hell. And she directly contradicted the slanderers, saying: "How could they eat their children, who may not eat blood even of creatures without reason?" And henceforth she confessed herself a Christian, and joined the inheritance of the martyrs.

Now when the tyrant's instruments of torture were brought to nought by Christ through the endurance of the blessed ones, the devil began to invent other devices: close confinement in prison, in darkness and its most noisome spot; stretching the feet in the stocks, and keeping them stretched five holes apart; and all those other torments which his servants when enraged—aye, and filled with their master—are wont to inflict upon prisoners. So that the more part were stifled in the prison, as many as the Lord willed thus to depart, that He might manifest His glory. For some, though tortured so cruelly that it seemed they could no longer live even with every attention, remained alive in the prison, destitute indeed of human care, but fortified afresh by the Lord and strengthened both in body and soul, cheering on and encouraging the rest. But others who were young and just recently apprehended, whose bodies had not been previously tortured, could not endure the rigour of their confinement, and died within its walls. Now the blessed Pothinus, to whom had been committed the ministry of the bishopric at Lyons, was above ninety years of age, and very weak in body. He was scarcely breathing because of the bodily weakness which was laid upon him, but the earnest desire for martyrdom filled him with that renewed strength which a willing spirit supplies. He too was haled to the tribunal, and though his body was weakened by both age and disease, his life was preserved within him, that through it Christ might triumph. He was conveyed to the tribunal by the soldiers, escorted by the city authorities and the whole multitude, who gave utterance to all sorts of cries, as if he were Christ Himself; and so he gave the good witness. Being examined by the governor as to who the God of the Christians was, he replied, "If thou art worthy, thou shalt know." And thereupon he was haled without mercy, and received blows of every kind: those close by heaped on him all manner of insult with blows of hands and feet, regardless of his age, while those at a distance made him the object of whatever missile came

Tradition holds that Christian martyrs waited in these underground rooms at the Colosseum before being sent to face lions in the arena.

to their hand. And all considered it a grievous fault and impiety to be behindhand in their wanton violence to him. For thus indeed they thought to avenge their gods. Scarcely breathing he was cast into prison, and after two days gave up the ghost.

Then in truth a mighty dispensation of God came to pass, and the measureless compassion of Jesus was displayed, in a manner rarely vouchsafed among the brethren, but not beyond the art of Christ. For they who had denied when the Christians were first arrested were also confined with [the others] and shared their sufferings; for on this occasion their denial had profited them nothing. On the contrary, those who confessed what they really were, were confined as Christians, no other charge being brought against them; while the others were detained thenceforward as murderers and scoundrels, and were punished twice as much as the rest. For the burden of the confessors was lightened by the joy of martyrdom, the hope of the promises, their love to Christ, and the Spirit of the Father. But the others were grievously tormented by their conscience, insomuch that their countenances could be clearly distinguished from all the rest as they passed by. For they went forth with joy, great glory and grace blended on their countenances, so that even their chains hung around them like a goodly ornament, as a bride adorned with golden fringes of divers colours, perfumed the while with the sweet savour of Christ; hence some supposed that they had been anointed with earthly ointment as well. But the others were dejected, downcast, unsightly and covered with every kind of confusion; reproached, moreover, by the heathen for baseness and cowardice; under the charge of murder, and having lost the one precious, glorious and life-giving Name. The rest beholding this were stablished, and those who were apprehended confessed without doubting, nor did they bestow even a thought upon the persuasion of the devil.
. . . After this their martyrdoms henceforth embraced every different form of death. For having woven a single crown of divers colours and variegated flowers they offered it to the Father. And so it was fitting that the noble champions, after having endured a varied conflict and mightily conquered, should receive as their due the mighty crown of incorruptibility. Maturus, then, and Sanctus and Blandina and Attalus were led to contend with wild beasts to the amphitheatre, and to the public spectacle of heathen inhumanity, a day for contests with wild beasts being granted of set purpose for our benefit. And Maturus and Sanctus passed

once more through every kind of torture in the amphitheatre, as if they had suffered absolutely nothing before, or rather as if they had already vanquished their antagonist in many rounds, and were now contending for the crown itself. Again they ran the gauntlet of scourges, as is the custom of the place. They were dragged by wild beasts; they endured all that the cries of a maddened populace ordered, now from this side, now from that; and last of all, the iron chair, which fried their bodies and choked them with smoke. Nor even at this point did the heathen stop, but were still further maddened, in their desire to conquer the Christians' endurance. Nevertheless nothing escaped the lips of Sanctus save that word of confession which it had been his wont from the very first to utter. So then, these men, whose life had lasted long through a mighty conflict, were finally sacrificed, being made throughout that day a spectacle unto the world in place of all the varied show that single combats offered.

Now Blandina, suspended on a stake, was exposed as food to wild beasts which were let loose against her. Even to look on her, as she hung cross-wise in earnest prayer, wrought great eagerness in those who were contending, for in their conflict they beheld with their outward eyes in the form of their sister Him who was crucified for them, that He might persuade those who believe in Him that all who suffer for the glory of Christ have unbroken fellowship with the living God. And as none of the wild beasts then touched her, she was taken down from the stake and cast again into prison, being kept for another conflict, that she might conquer in still further contests, and so both render irrevocable the sentence passed on the crooked serpent, and encourage the brethren—she the small, the weak, the despised, who had put on Christ the great and invincible Champion, and who in many rounds vanquished the adversary and through conflict was crowned with the crown of incorruptibility.

As for Attalus, he too was loudly called for by the crowd (for he was well known), and entered the arena a ready combatant by reason of his good conscience, since he had been truly exercised in the Christian discipline, and always a witness among us of truth. He was conducted round the amphitheatre, preceded by a board, on which was written in Latin "This is Attalus the Christian," the people bursting with vehement indignation against him. But when the governor learnt that he was a Roman, he ordered him to be taken back to the prison, where also were the others concerning whom he wrote to Caesar and was awaiting his sentence.

But the intervening time proved not idle nor unfruitful in their case; nay, through their endurance the measureless compassion of Christ was displayed. For by the living the dead were quickened, and martyrs forgave those who were not martyrs, and the virgin mother rejoiced greatly to receive alive those whom her womb had brought forth dead. For by their means the more part of those who had denied were brought again to birth, were conceived again, were rekindled into life, and learnt to confess. Full now of life and vigour they approached the tribunal, for their trial was made sweet by God, who hath no pleasure in the death of the sinner, but is kind towards repentance; that they might be again questioned by the governor. For Caesar had written that they should be tortured to death, but that any who denied should be set free. And as the national festival held in that place was then at its commencement—a festival largely attended by visitors from all the tribes—the governor had the blessed ones conducted to the tribunal, to make of them a spectacle, and to form a procession for the benefit of the crowds. Therefore he again examined them; and those who appeared to possess Roman citizenship he beheaded, but sent the others to the wild beasts. And Christ was mightily glorified in those who formerly denied Him, but then confessed, contrary to the expectation of the heathen. Indeed they were examined by themselves, presumably as a prelude to their release; but confessing, were added to the inheritance of the martyrs. And there remained outside those who had never even a trace of faith, or an idea of the marriage garment, or a thought for the fear of God, nay rather, blaspheming the Way by their manner of life—in fact, the sons of perdition. But all the rest were added to the Church.

While these were being examined, a certain Alexander, a Phrygian by race and a physician by profession, who had lived for many years in the Gauls, and was known almost to everyone for his love to God and boldness for the word (for he too was not destitute of the apostolic gift), stood by the tribunal and by signs encouraged them to confess. To the bystanders there he appeared to be, as it were, in travail. The crowd were enraged that those who had formerly denied should afterwards confess, and cried out against Alexander as the cause of this. Thereupon the

St. Stephen's Gate in a Jerusalem city wall is named for the first Christian martyr.

governor summoned him and asked him who he was; and angry at his reply "A Christian," condemned him to the wild beasts. And on the following day he entered [the amphitheatre] in the company of Attalus as well; for indeed the governor, to please the crowd, had delivered Attalus too again to the wild beasts. These men experienced in turn every instrument that has been devised for torture in the amphitheatre, and, having endured a mighty conflict, at last were sacrificed like the rest. Alexander neither groaned nor uttered the slightest cry, but held converse with God in his heart. But Attalus, when he was placed in the iron chair and scorched, so that the fumes rose from his body, addressed the multitude in Latin: "Behold, this which ye do is devouring men; but we neither devour men nor practise any other wickedness." And on being asked the name of God, he replied, "God has not a name as a man has." And after all these, finally on the last day of the single combats Blandina was again brought in, in the company of Ponticus, a lad about fifteen years old. They had also been fetched in every day to view the tortures of the others. The heathen tried to force them to swear by their idols, and as they remained firm and set them at nought, the multitude was so infuriated at them that it had neither compassion for the youth of the boy nor respect for the sex of the woman. Nay, they exposed them to every cruelty and brought them through the entire round of tortures, again and again trying to force them to swear. But this they were unable to accomplish; for Ponticus, encouraged by his sister (so that the heathen themselves saw that it was she who was urging him on and strengthening him), having nobly endured every kind of torture gave up his spirit. But the blessed Blandina last of all, having, like a high-born mother, exhorted her children and sent them forth victorious to the King, travelled herself along the same path of conflicts as they did, and hastened to them, rejoicing and exulting at her departure, like one bidden to a marriage supper, rather than cast to the wild beasts. And after the scourging, after the wild beasts, after the frying-pan, she was at last thrown into a basket and presented to a bull. For a time the animal tossed her, but she had now lost all perception of what was happening, thanks to the hope she cherished, her grasp of the objects of her faith, and her intercourse with Christ. Then she too was sacrificed, and even the heathen themselves acknowledged that never in their experience had a woman endured so many terrible sufferings.

A Christian woman given to the lions in the Roman amphitheater.

Nevertheless not even thus were their madness and cruelty towards the saints satisfied. For wild and barbarous tribes when incited by a wild beast were not easily checked; and their wanton violence found another distinct outlet with regard to the corpses. That they had been worsted did not put them out of countenance, since for them man's gift of reason did not exist. Nay rather, in them as in a wild beast the fact inflamed anger, and the governor and people were at one in displaying an unjust hatred towards us, that the Scripture might be fulfilled: He that is lawless, let him do lawlessness still: and he that is righteous, let him be accounted righteous still. For indeed they cast those suffocated in prison to the dogs, and kept a careful guard by night and day lest any should receive funeral rites at our hands. And then they actually exposed what the wild beasts and the fire had left behind— mangled or charred, as the case might be—and the heads of the others together with their severed trunks, and guarded them likewise from burial, with a military watch, for many days. And some were moved with indignation and gnashed on them with their teeth, seeking to take still further vengeance upon them; while others laughed and jeered, at the same time exalting their own idols, to whom they attributed the punishment of the Christians. Others again, of a more forbearing nature and seeming to extend to them a measure of fellow-feeling, uttered many reproaches, saying, "Where is their God? and what profit has their religion brought them, which they have preferred to their own life?" So varied, then, was their attitude; but as for us, we were plunged in great grief, in that we could not bury the bodies in the earth. For neither did night avail us for this purpose, nor did money persuade or prayers move them. But in every possible way they kept guard, as if the prevention of burial would bring them great gain.

. . . The bodies, then, of the martyrs, which for six days were displayed and exposed to the elements in every way possible, the lawless men afterwards burnt and reduced to ashes. Then they swept them down into the river Rhone which flows close by, so that not even a trace of them might remain upon the earth. And this they did, thinking that they could conquer God and deprive them of the regeneration, "in order," as they themselves said, "that they may not even have hope of a resurrection, in faith of which they introduce into our midst a certain strange and new-fangled cult, and despise dread torments, and are ready to go to their death, and that too with joy. Now let us see if they will rise again, and if their god can help them, and deliver them out of our hands." (Lawlor and Oulton, *Eusebius,* I, pp. 140–7, slightly altered.)

While some practice of religion is permitted in communist countries today, it was actively persecuted for many years and is still discouraged. As a result, many of the Russian Orthodox churches in the Soviet Union, such as St. Basil's on Red Square in Moscow, are no longer permitted to be used as churches.

READING 8

Letter from a Young Communist*

"What seems of first importance to you is to me either not desirable or impossible of realization. But there is one thing about which I am in dead earnest—and that is the socialist cause. It is my life, my business, my religion, my hobby, my sweetheart, wife, and mistress, my bread and meat. I work at it in the daytime and dream of it at night. Its hold on me grows, not lessens, as time goes on. I'll be in it the rest of my life. It is my alter-ego. When you think of me, it is necessary to think of socialism as well, because I'm inseparably bound to it.

"Therefore I can't carry on a friendship, a love affair, or even a conversation without relating it to this force which both drives and guides my life. I evaluate people, books, ideas, and notions according to how they affect the socialist cause and by their attitude toward it.

"I have already been in jail because of my ideas, and if necessary I am ready to go before a firing squad. A certain percentage of us get killed or imprisoned. Even for those who escape these harsher ends, life is no bed of roses. A genuine radical lives in virtual poverty. He turns back to the party every penny he makes above what is absolutely necessary to keep him alive. We constantly look for places where the class struggle is the sharpest,

*From *Presbyterian Survey* (February 1961), p. 1.

exploiting these situations to the limit of their possibilities. We lead strikes. We organize demonstrations. We speak on street corners. We fight cops. We go through trying experiences many times each year which the ordinary man has to face only once or twice in a lifetime.

"And when we're not doing these more exciting things, all our spare time is taken up with dull routine chores, endless leg work, errands, etc., which are inescapably connected with running a live organization.

"Radicals don't have the time or the money for many movies or concerts or T-bone steaks or decent homes and new cars. We've been described as fanatics. We are. Our lives are dominated by one great, overshadowing factor—the struggle for socialism.

"Well, that's what my life is going to be. That's the black side of it. Then there is the other side of it. We communists have a philosophy of life which no amount of money could buy. We have a cause to fight for, a definite purpose in life. We subordinate our petty personal selves into a great movement of humanity. We have a morale, an *esprit de corps* such as no capitalist army ever had; we have a code of conduct, a way of life, a devotion to our cause that no religious order can touch. And we are guided not by blind, fanatical faith but by logic and reason, by a never-ending education of study and practice.

"And if our personal lives seem hard or our egos appear to suffer through subordination to the party, then we are adequately compensated by the thought that each of us is in his small way helping to contribute something new and true, something better to mankind."

READING 9

The Lord's Prayer

*The following version of the Lord's Prayer is taken from Matthew 6:9–13.**

Pray then like this:

Our Father who art in heaven,
Hallowed be thy name.
Thy kingdom come,
Thy will be done,
  On earth as it is in heaven.
Give us this day our daily bread;
And forgive us our debts,
  As we also have forgiven our debtors;
And lead us not into temptation,
  But deliver us from evil.

Another version is found in Luke 11:2-4.

And he said to them, "When you pray, say:

"Father, hallowed be thy name. Thy
kingdom come. Give us each day our
daily bread; and forgive us our
sins, for we ourselves forgive every one
who is indebted to us; and lead us not
into temptation."

*This passage and the following passage from Luke are from *The Common Bible,* Revised Standard Version (New York: William Collins Sons, 1973).

The following is a recent translation of the Lord's Prayer. *

Our Father in heaven,
　　hallowed be your Name,
　　your kingdom come,
　　your will be done,
　　　　on earth as in heaven.
Give us today our daily bread.
Forgive us our sins
　　as we forgive whose who sin against us.
Save us from the time of trial
　　and deliver us from evil.
For the kingdom, the power, and the glory are yours
　　now and for ever.

The Lord's Prayer lies at the heart of the Christian devotion; and it is laden with rich personal and traditional associations. Change therefore prompts all kinds of reactions. But change is no new thing in the history of this prayer, and today no single invariable version is in common use throughout the English-speaking world. Comparison of the text of Matt. 6:9–13 in the Authorized Version of the Bible with the version in the Anglican Book of Common Prayer of 1662 at once reveals differences. Such variations may serve to remind us that between our current and familiar versions and the Greek text of the prayer, as recorded in the New Testament, stand earlier English renderings and an even earlier Latin translation. To retranslate the Lord's Prayer for a new situation is no new procedure. It should also be emphasized that in the task of producing translations the church has never been in the position of working from and with one fixed "original" text. It is clear that the Greek texts of the prayer as preserved in the Gospels are themselves a "translation" from Hebrew or Aramaic, and the texts which appear in Matthew and Luke do not agree. . . .

The new translation of the Greek text which is offered is mainly based on that in St. Matthew's Gospel, since this has always been the basis of the church's liturgical tradition. It retains the style and even the words of the familiar version so far as this is consistent with the elimination of archaic expressions and with the demands of clear and accurate translation.

---

*This version and the explanation that follows it are from *Prayers We Have in Common* (pp. 1–2).

READING 10

The Virgin Birth of Jesus Christ

Illuminated Bible manuscript painting shows the Adoration of Jesus by the wise men.

Matthew 1:18–25*

Now the birth of Jesus Christ took place in this way. When his mother Mary had been betrothed to Joseph, before they came together she was found to be with child of the Holy Spirit; and her husband Joseph, being a just man and unwilling to put her to shame, resolved to divorce her quietly. But as he considered this, behold, an angel of the Lord appeared to him in a dream, saying, "Joseph, son of David, do not fear to take Mary your wife, for that which is conceived in her is of the Holy Spirit; she will bear a son, and you shall call his name Jesus, for he will save his people from their sins." All this took place to fulfill what the Lord had spoken by the prophet:

"Behold, a virgin shall conceive and bear a son,
and his name shall be called Emman′-u-el "

(which means, God with us). When Joseph woke from sleep, he did as the angel of the Lord commanded him; he took his wife, but knew her not until she had borne a son; and he called his name Jesus.

*From *The Common Bible,* Revised Standard Version.

This fresco in a modern German Catholic church depicts John's baptism of Jesus in the River Jordan. The rays behind Jesus symbolize the Father's presence; the dove symbolizes the presence of the Holy Ghost.

READING 11

The Gospel According to Mark*

A. Mark 1–8:30

1 The beginning of the gospel of Jesus Christ, the Son of God.
As it is written in Isaiah the prophet,
"Behold, I send my messenger before thy face,
who shall prepare thy way;
the voice of one crying in the wilderness:
Prepare the way of the Lord,
make his paths straight—"
John the baptizer appeared in the wilderness, preaching a baptism of repentance for the forgiveness of sins. And there went out to him all the country of Judea, and all the people of Jerusalem; and they were baptized by him in the river Jordan, confessing their sins. Now John was clothed with camel's hair, and had a leather girdle around his waist, and ate locusts and wild honey. And he preached, saying, "After me comes he who is mightier than I, the thong of whose sandals I am not worthy to stoop down and untie. I have baptized you with water; but he will baptize you with the Holy Spirit."
In those days Jesus came from Nazareth of Galilee and was baptized by John in the Jordan. And when he came up out of the

*From *The Common Bible*, Revised Standard Version.

water, immediately he saw the heavens opened and the Spirit descending upon him like a dove; and a voice came from heaven, "Thou art my beloved Son; with thee I am well pleased."

The Spirit immediately drove him out into the wilderness. And he was in the wilderness forty days, tempted by Satan; and he was with the wild beasts; and the angels ministered to him.

Now after John was arrested, Jesus came into Galilee, preaching the gospel of God, and saying, "The time is fulfilled, and the kingdom of God is at hand; repent, and believe in the gospel."

And passing along by the Sea of Galilee, he saw Simon and Andrew the brother of Simon casting a net in the sea; for they were fishermen. And Jesus said to them, "Follow me and I will make you become fishers of men." And immediately they left their nets and followed him. And going on a little farther, he saw James the son of Zeb'edee and John his brother, who were in their boat mending the nets. And immediately he called them; and they left their father Zeb'edee in the boat with the hired servants, and followed him.

The apostles played an important role in the spread of Christianity and were in turn honored by the early Christians. This sculpture of them decorated a tomb in southern France in Roman times.

And they went into Caper'na-um; and immediately on the sabbath he entered the synagogue and taught. And they were astonished at his teaching, for he taught them as one who had authority, and not as the scribes. And immediately there was in their synagogue a man with an unclean spirit; and he cried out, "What have you to do with us, Jesus of Nazareth? Have you come to destroy us? I know who you are, the Holy One of God." But Jesus rebuked him, saying, "Be silent, and come out of him!" And the unclean spirit, convulsing him and crying with a loud voice, came out of him. And they were all amazed, so that they questioned among themselves, saying, "What is this? A new teaching! With authority he commands even the unclean spirits, and they obey him." And at once his fame spread everywhere throughout all the surrounding region of Galilee.

And immediately he left the synagogue, and entered the house of Simon and Andrew, with James and John. Now Simon's mother-in-law lay sick with a fever, and immediately they told him of her. And he came and took her by the hand and lifted her up, and the fever left her; and she served them.

That evening, at sundown, they brought to him all who were sick or possessed with demons. And the whole city was gathered together about the door. And he healed many who were sick with various diseases, and cast out many demons; and he would not permit the demons to speak, because they knew him.

And in the morning, a great while before day, he rose and went out to a lonely place, and there he prayed. And Simon and those who were with him pursued him, and they found him and said to him, "Every one is searching for you." And he said to them, "Let us go on to the next towns, that I may preach there also; for that is why I came out." And he went throughout all Galilee, preaching in their synagogues and casting out demons.

And a leper came to him, beseeching him, and kneeling said to him, "If you will, you can make me clean." Moved with pity, he stretched out his hand and touched him, and said to him, "I will; be clean." And immediately the leprosy left him, and he was made clean. And he sternly charged him, and sent him away at once, and said to him, "See that you say nothing to any one; but go, show yourself to the priest, and offer for your cleansing what Moses commanded, for a proof to the people." But he went out and began to talk freely about it, and to spread the news, so that Jesus could no longer openly enter a town, but was out in the country; and people came to him from every quarter.

2 And when he returned to Caper'na-um after some days, it was reported that he was at home. And many were gathered together, so that there was no longer room for them, not even about the door; and he was preaching the word to them. And they came, bringing to him a paralytic carried by four men. And when they could not get near him because of the crowd, they removed the roof above him; and when they had made an opening, they let down the pallet on which the paralytic lay. And when Jesus saw their faith, he said to the paralytic, "My son, your sins are forgiven." Now some of the scribes were sitting there, questioning in their hearts, "Why does this man speak thus? It is blasphemy! Who can forgive sins but God alone?" And immediately Jesus, perceiving in his spirit that they thus questioned within themselves, said to them, "Why do you question thus in your hearts? Which is easier, to say to the paralytic, 'Your sins are forgiven,' or to say, 'Rise, take up your pallet and walk'? But that you may know that the Son of man has authority on earth to forgive sins"—he said to the paralytic—"I say to you, rise, take up your pallet and go home." And he rose, and immediately took up the pallet and went out before them all; so that they were all amazed and glorified God, saying, "We never saw anything like this!"

He went out again beside the sea; and all the crowd gathered about him, and he taught them. And as he passed on, he saw Levi the son of Alphaeus sitting at the tax office, and he said to him, "Follow me." And he rose and followed him.

And as he sat at table in his house, many tax collectors and sinners were sitting with Jesus and his disciples; for there were many who followed him. And the scribes of the Pharisees, when they saw that he was eating with sinners and tax collectors, said to his disciples, "Why does he eat with tax collectors and sinners?" And when Jesus heard it, he said to them, "Those who are well have no need of a physician, but those who are sick; I came not to call the righteous, but sinners."

Now John's disciples and the Pharisees were fasting; and people came and said to him, "Why do John's disciples and the disciples of the Pharisees fast, but your disciples do not fast?" And Jesus said to them, "Can the wedding guests fast while the bridegroom is with them? As long as they have the bridegroom with them, they cannot fast. The days will come, when the bridegroom is taken away from them, and then they will fast in that day. No one sews a piece of unshrunk cloth on an old garment; if he does, the patch tears away from it, the new from the old, and a worse tear is made. And no one puts new wine into old wineskins; if he does, the wine will burst the skins, and the wine is lost, and so are the skins; but new wine is for fresh skins."

One sabbath he was going through the grainfields; and as they made their way his disciples began to pluck heads of grain. And the Pharisees said to him, "Look, why are they doing what is not lawful on the sabbath?" And he said to them, "Have you never read what David did, when he was in need and was hungry, he and those who were with him: how he entered the house of God, when Abi'athar was high priest, and ate the bread of the Presence, which it is not lawful for any but the priests to eat, and also gave it to those who were with him?" And he said to them, "The sabbath was made for man, not man for the sabbath; so the Son of man is lord even of the sabbath."

3 Again he entered the synagogue, and a man was there who had a withered hand. And they watched him, to see whether he would heal him on the sabbath, so that they might accuse him. And he said to the man who had the withered hand, "Come here." And he said to them, "Is it lawful on the sabbath to do good or to do harm, to save life or to kill?" But they were silent. And he looked around at them with anger, grieved at their hardness of heart, and said to the man, "Stretch out your hand." He stretched it out, and his hand was restored. The Pharisees went out, and immediately held counsel with the Hero'di-ans against him, how to destroy him.

Jesus withdrew with his disciples to the sea, and a great multitude from Galilee followed; also from Judea and Jerusalem and Idume'a and from beyond the Jordan and from about Tyre and Sidon a great multitude, hearing all that he did, came to him. And he told his disciples to have a boat ready for him because of the crowd, lest.they should crush him; for he had healed many, so that all who had diseases pressed upon him to touch him. And whenever the unclean spirits beheld him, they fell down before him and cried out, "You are the Son of God." And he strictly ordered them not to make him known.

And he went up on the mountain, and called to him those whom he desired; and they came to him. And he appointed twelve, to be with him, and to be sent out to preach and have authority to cast out demons: Simon whom he surnamed Peter; James the son of Zeb'edee and John the brother of James, whom he surnamed Bo-aner'ges, that is, sons of thunder; Andrew, and Philip, and Bartholomew, and Matthew, and Thomas, and James the son of Alphaeus, and Thaddaeus, and Simon the Cananaean, and Judas Iscariot, who betrayed him.

Then he went home; and the crowd came together again, so that they could not even eat. And when his family heard it, they went out to seize him, for people were saying, "He is beside himself." And the scribes who came down from Jerusalem said, "He is possessed by Be-el'zebub, and by the prince of demons he casts out the demons." And he called them to him, and said to them in parables, "How can Satan cast out Satan? If a kingdom is divided against itself, that kingdom cannot stand. And if a house is divided against itself, that house will not be able to stand. And if Satan has risen up against himself and is divided, he cannot stand, but is coming to an end. But no one can enter a strong man's house and plunder his goods, unless he first binds the strong man; then indeed he may plunder his house.

"Truly, I say to you, all sins will be forgiven the sons of men, and whatever blasphemies they utter; but whoever blasphemes against the Holy Spirit never has forgiveness, but is guilty of an eternal sin"—for they had said, "He has an unclean spirit."

And his mother and his brothers came; and standing outside they sent to him and called him. And a crowd was sitting about him; and they said to him, "Your mother and your brothers are outside, asking for you." And he replied, "Who are my mother and my brothers?" And looking around, on those who sat about him, he said, "Here are my mother and my brothers! Whoever does the will of God is my brother, and sister, and mother."

4 Again he began to teach beside the sea. And a very large crowd gathered about him, so that he got into a boat and sat in it on the sea; and the whole crowd was beside the sea on the land. And he taught them many things in parables, and in his teaching he said to them: "Listen! A sower went out to sow. And as he sowed, some seed fell along the path, and the birds came and devoured it. Other seed fell on rocky ground, where it had not much soil, and immediately it sprang up, since it had no depth of soil; and when the sun rose it was scorched, and since it had no root it withered away. Other seed fell among thorns and the thorns grew up and choked it, and it yielded no grain. And other seeds fell into good soil and brought forth grain, growing up and increasing and yielding thirtyfold and sixtyfold and a hundredfold." And he said, "He who has ears to hear, let him hear."

And when he was alone, those who were about him with the twelve asked him concerning the parables. And he said to them, "To you has been given the secret of the kingdom of God, but for those outside everything is in parables; so that they may indeed see but not perceive, and may indeed hear but not understand; lest they should turn again, and be forgiven." And he said to them, "Do you not understand this parable? How then will you understand all the parables? The sower sows the word. And these are the ones along the path, where the word is sown; when they hear, Satan immediately comes and takes away the word which is sown in them. And these in like manner are the ones sown upon rocky ground, who, when they hear the word, immediately receive it with joy; and they have no root in themselves, but endure for a while; then, when tribulation or persecution arises on account of the word, immediately they fall away. And others are the ones who hear the word, but the cares of the world, and the delight in riches,

This fresco from a German Catholic church shows Jesus and disciples in the Storm at Sea.

and the desire for other things, enter in and choke the word, and it proves unfruitful. But those that were sown upon the good soil are the ones who hear the word and accept it and bear fruit, thirtyfold and sixtyfold and a hundredfold."

And he said to them, "Is a lamp brought in to be put under a bushel, or under a bed, and not on a stand? For there is nothing hid, except to be made manifest; nor is anything secret, except to come to light. If any man has ears to hear, let him hear." And he said to them, "Take heed what you hear; the measure you give will be the measure you get, and still more will be given you. For to him who has will more be given; and from him who has not, even what he has will be taken away."

And he said, "The kingdom of God is as if a man should scatter seed upon the ground, and should sleep and rise night and day, and the seed should sprout and grow, he knows not how. The earth produces of itself, first the blade, then the ear, then the full grain in the ear. But when the grain is ripe, at once he puts in the sickle, because the harvest has come."

And he said, "With what can we compare the kingdom of God, or what parable shall we use for it? It is like a grain of mustard seed, which, when sown upon the ground, is the smallest of all the seeds on earth; yet when it is sown it grows up and becomes the greatest of all shrubs, and puts forth large branches, so that the birds of the air can make nests in its shade."

With many such parables he spoke the word to them, as they were able to hear it; he did not speak to them without a parable, but privately to his own disciples he explained everything.

On that day, when evening had come, he said to them, "Let us go across to the other side." And leaving the crowd, they took him with them in the boat, just as he was. And other boats were with him. And a great storm of wind arose, and the waves beat into the boat, so that the boat was already filling. But he was in the stern, asleep on the cushion; and they woke him and said to him, "Teacher, do you not care if we perish?" And he awoke and rebuked the wind, and said to the sea, "Peace! Be still!" And the wind ceased, and there was a great calm. He said to them, "Why are you afraid? Have you no faith?" And they were filled with awe, and said to one another, "Who then is this, that even wind and sea obey him?"

5 They came to the other side of the sea, to the country of the Ger'asenes. And when he had come out of the boat, there met him out of the tombs a man with an unclean spirit, who lived among the tombs; and no one could bind him any more, even with a chain; for he had often been bound with fetters and chains, but the chains he wrenched apart, and the fetters he broke in pieces; and no one had the strength to subdue him. Night and day among the tombs and on the mountains he was always crying out, and bruising himself with stones. And when he saw Jesus from afar, he ran and worshiped him; and crying out with a loud voice, he said, "What have you to do with me, Jesus, Son of the Most High God? I adjure you by God, do not torment me." For he had said to him, "Come out of the man, you unclean spirit!" And Jesus asked him, "What is your name?" He replied, "My name is Legion; for we are many." And he begged him eagerly not to send them out of the country. Now a great herd of swine was feeding there on the hillside; and they begged him, "Send us to the swine, let us enter them." So he gave them leave. And the unclean spirits came out, and entered the swine; and the herd, numbering about two thousand, rushed down the steep bank into the sea, and were drowned in the sea.

The herdsman fled, and told it in the city and in the country. And people came to see what it was that had happened. And they came to Jesus, and saw the demoniac sitting there, clothed and in his right mind, the man who had had the legion; and they were afraid. And those who had seen it told what had happened to the demoniac and to the swine. And they began to beg Jesus to depart from their neighborhood. And as he was getting into the boat, the man who had been possessed with demons begged him that he might be with him. But he refused, and said to him, "Go home to your friends, and tell them how much the Lord has done for you, and how he has had mercy on you." And he went away and began to proclaim in the Decap'olis how much Jesus had done for him; and all men marveled.

And when Jesus had crossed again in the boat to the other side, a great crowd gathered about him; and he was beside the sea. Then came one of the rulers of the synagogue, Ja'irus by name; and seeing him, he fell at his feet, and besought him, saying, "My little daughter is at the point of death. Come and lay your hands on her, so that she may be made well, and live." And he went with him.

And a great crowd followed him and thronged about him. And there was a woman who had had a flow of blood for twelve years, and who had suffered much under many physicians, and had spent all that she had, and was no better but rather grew worse. She had heard the reports about Jesus, and came up behind him in the crowd and touched his garment. For she said, "If I touch even his garments, I shall be made well." And immediately the hemorrhage ceased; and she felt in her body that she was healed of her disease. And Jesus, perceiving in himself that power had gone forth from him, immediately turned about in the crowd, and said, "Who touched my garments?" And his disciples said to him, "You see the crowd pressing around you, and yet you say, 'Who touched me?'" And he looked around to see who had done it. But the woman, knowing what had been done to her, came in fear and trembling and fell down before him, and told him the whole truth. And he said to her, "Daughter, your faith has made you well; go in peace, and be healed of your disease."

While he was still speaking, there came from the ruler's house some who said, "Your daughter is dead. Why trouble the Teacher any further?" But ignoring what they said, Jesus said to the ruler of the synagogue, "Do not fear, only believe." And he allowed no one to follow him except Peter and James and John the brother of James. When they came to the house of the ruler of the synagogue, he saw a tumult, and people weeping and wailing loudly. And when he had entered, he said to them, "Why do you make a tumult and weep? The child is not dead but sleeping." And they laughed at him. But he put them all outside, and took the child's father and mother and those who were with him, and went in where the child was. Taking her by the hand he said to her, "Tal'itha cu'mi"; which means, "Little girl, I say to you, arise." And immediately the girl got up and walked (she was twelve years of age), and they were immediately overcome with amazement. And he strictly charged them that no one should know this, and told them to give her something to eat.

6 He went away from there and came to his own country; and his disciples followed him. And on the sabbath he began to teach in the synagogue; and many who heard him were astonished, saying, "Where did this man get all this? What is the wisdom given to him? What mighty works are wrought by his hands! Is not this the carpenter, the son of Mary and brother of

James and Joses and Judas and Simon, and are not his sisters here with us?" And they took offense at him. And Jesus said to them, "A prophet is not without honor, except in his own country, and among his own kin, and in his own house." And he could do no mighty work there, except that he laid his hands upon a few sick people and healed them. And he marveled because of their unbelief.

And he went about among the villages teaching.

And he called to him the twelve, and began to send them out two by two, and gave them authority over the unclean spirits. He charged them to take nothing for their journey except a staff; no bread, no bag, no money in their belts; but to wear sandals and not put on two tunics. And he said to them, "Where you enter a house, stay there until you leave the place. And if any place will not receive you and they refuse to hear you, when you leave, shake off the dust that is on your feet for a testimony against them." So they went out and preached that men should repent. And they cast out many demons, and anointed with oil many that were sick and healed them.

King Herod heard of it; for Jesus' name had become known. Some said, "John the baptizer has been raised from the dead; that is why these powers are at work in him." But others said, "It is Eli'jah." And others said, "It is a prophet, like one of the prophets of old." But when Herod heard of it he said, "John, whom I beheaded, has been raised." For Herod had sent and seized John, and bound him in prison for the sake of Hero'di-as, his brother Philip's wife; because he had married her. For John said to Herod, "It is not lawful for you to have your brother's wife." And Hero'di-as had a grudge against him, and wanted to kill him. But she could not, for Herod feared John, knowing that he was a righteous and holy man, and kept him safe. When he heard him, he was much perplexed; and yet he heard him gladly. But an opportunity came when Herod on his birthday gave a banquet for his courtiers and officers and the leading men of Galilee. For when Hero'di-as' daughter came in and danced, she pleased Herod and his guests; and the king said to the girl, "Ask me for whatever you wish, and I will grant it." And he vowed to her, "Whatever you ask me, I will give you, even half of my kingdom." And she went out, and said to her mother, "What shall I ask?" And she said, "The head of John the baptizer." And she came in immediately with haste to the king, and asked, saying, "I want you to give me at once the head of John the Baptist on a platter." And the king was exceedingly sorry; but because of his oaths and his guests he did not want to break his word to her. And immediately the king sent a soldier of the guard and gave orders to bring his head. He went and beheaded him in the prison, and brought his head on a platter, and gave it to the girl; and the girl gave it to her mother. When his disciples heard of it, they came and took his body, and laid it in a tomb.

The apostles returned to Jesus, and told him all that they had done and taught. And he said to them, "Come away by yourselves to a lonely place, and rest a while." For many were coming and going, and they had no leisure even to eat. And they went away in the boat to a lonely place by themselves. Now many saw them going, and knew them, and they ran there on foot from all the towns, and got there ahead of them. As he went ashore he saw a great throng, and he had compassion on them, because they were like sheep without a shepherd; and he began to teach them many things. And when it grew late, his disciples came to him and said, "This is a lonely place, and the hour is now late; send them away, to go into the country and villages round about and buy them-selves something to eat." But he answered them, "You give them something to eat." And they said to him, "Shall we go and buy two hundred denarii worth of bread, and give it to them to eat?" And he said to them, "How many loaves have you? Go and see." And when they had found out, they said, "Five, and two fish." Then he commanded them all to sit down by companies upon the green grass. So they sat down in groups, by hundreds and by fifties. And taking the five loaves and the two fish he looked up to heaven, and blessed, and broke the loaves, and gave them to the disciples to set before the people; and he divided the two fish among them all. And they all ate and were satisfied. And they took up twelve baskets full of broken pieces and of the fish. And those who ate the loaves were five thousand men.

Immediately he made his disciples get into the boat and go before him to the other side, to Beth-sa'ida, while he dismissed the crowd. And after he had taken leave of them, he went up on the mountain to pray. And when evening came, the boat was out on the sea, and he was alone on the land. And he saw that they were making headway painfully, for the wind was against them. And about the fourth watch of the night he came to them, walking on the sea. He meant to pass by them, but when they saw him walking on the sea they thought it was a ghost, and cried out; for

A mosaic of the loaves and fishes with which Jesus fed the multitude.

they all saw him, and were terrified. But immediately he spoke to them and said, "Take heart, it is I; have no fear." And he got into the boat with them and the wind ceased. And they were utterly astounded, for they did not understand about the loaves, but their hearts were hardened.

And when they had crossed over, they came to land at Gennes'aret, and moored to the shore. And when they got out of the boat, immediately the people recognized him, and ran about the whole neighborhood and began to bring sick people on their pallets to any place where they heard he was. And wherever he came, in villages, cities, or country, they laid the sick in the market places, and besought him that they might touch even the fringe of his garment; and as many as touched it were made well.

7 Now when the Pharisees gathered together to him, with some of the scribes, who had come from Jerusalem, they saw that some of his disciples ate with hands defiled, that is, unwashed. (For the Pharisees, and all the Jews, do not eat unless they wash their hands, observing the tradition of the elders; and when they come from the market place, they do not eat unless they purify themselves; and there are many other traditions which they observe, the washing of cups and pots and vessels of bronze.) And the Pharisees and the scribes asked him, "Why do your disciples not live according to the tradition of the elders, but eat with hands defiled?" And he said to them, "Well did Isaiah prophesy of you hypocrites, as it is written,

'This people honors me with their lips,
but their heart is far from me;
in vain do they worship me,
teaching as doctrines the precepts of men.'
You leave the commandment of God, and hold fast the tradition of men."

And he said to them, "You have a fine way of rejecting the commandment of God, in order to keep your tradition! For Moses said, 'Honor your father and your mother'; and, 'He who speaks evil of father or mother, let him surely die'; but you say, 'If a man tells his father or his mother, What you would have gained from me is Corban' (that is, given to God)—then you no longer permit him to do anything for his father or mother, thus making void the word of God through your tradition which you hand on. And many such things you do."

And he called the people to him again, and said to them, "Hear me, all of you, and understand: there is nothing outside a man which by going into him can defile him; but the things which come out of a man are what defile him." And when he had entered the house, and left the people, his disciples asked him about the parable. And he said to them, "Then are you also without understanding? Do you not see that whatever goes into a man from outside cannot defile him, since it enters, not his heart but his stomach, and so passes on?" (Thus he declared all foods clean.) And he said, "What comes out of a man is what defiles a man. For from within, out of the heart of man, come evil thoughts, fornication, theft, murder, adultery, coveting, wickedness, deceit, licentiousness, envy, slander, pride, foolishness. All these evil things come from within, and they defile a man."

And from there he arose and went away to the region of Tyre and Sidon. And he entered a house, and would not have any one know it; yet he could not be hid. But immediately a woman, whose little daughter was possessed by an unclean spirit, heard of him, and came and fell down at his feet. Now the woman was a Greek, a Syrophoeni'cian by birth. And she begged him to cast the demon out of her daughter. And he said to her, "Let the children first be fed, for it is not right to take the children's bread and throw it to the dogs." But she answered him, "Yes, Lord; yet even the dogs under the table eat the children's crumbs." And he said to her, "For this saying you may go your way; the demon has left your daughter." And she went home, and found the child lying in bed, and the demon gone.

Then he returned from the region of Tyre, and went through Sidon to the Sea of Galilee, through the region of the Decap'olis. And they brought to him a man who was deaf and had an impediment in his speech; and they besought him to lay his hand upon him. And taking him aside from the multitude privately, he put his fingers into his ears, and he spat and touched his tongue; and looking up to heaven, he sighed, and said to him, "Eph-'phatha," that is, "Be opened." And his ears were opened, his tongue was released, and he spoke plainly. And he charged them to tell no one; but the more he charged them, the more zealously they proclaimed it. And they were astonished beyond measure, saying, "He has done all things well; he even makes the deaf hear and the dumb speak."

8 In those days, when again a great crowd had gathered, and they had nothing to eat, he called his disciples to him, and said to them, "I have compassion on the crowd, because they have been with me now three days, and have nothing to eat; and if I send them away hungry to their homes, they will faint on the way; and some of them have come a long way." And his disciples answered him, "How can one feed these men with bread here in the desert?" And he said to them, "How many loaves have you?" They said, "Seven." And he commanded the crowd to sit down on the ground; and he took the seven loaves, and having given thanks he broke them and gave them to his disciples to set before the people; and they set them before the crowd. And they had a few small fish; and having blessed them, he commanded that these also should be set before them. And they ate, and were satisfied; and they took up the broken pieces left over, seven baskets full. And there were about four thousand people. And he sent them away; and immediately he got into the boat with his disciples, and went to the district of Dalmanu'tha.

The Pharisees came and began to argue with him, seeking from him a sign from heaven, to test him. And he sighed deeply in his spirit, and said, "Why does this generation seek a sign? Truly, I say to you, no sign shall be given to this generation." And he left them, and getting into the boat again he departed to the other side.

Now they had forgotten to bring bread; and they had only one loaf with them in the boat. And he cautioned them, saying, "Take heed, beware of the leaven of the Pharisees and the leaven of Herod." And they discussed it with one another, saying, "We have no bread." And being aware of it, Jesus said to them, "Why do you discuss the fact that you have no bread? Do you not yet perceive or understand? Are your hearts hardened? Having eyes do you not see, and having ears do you not hear? And do you not remember? When I broke the five loaves for the five thousand, how many baskets full of broken pieces did you take up?" They said to him, "Twelve." "And the seven for the four thousand, how many baskets full of broken pieces did you take up?" And they said to him, "Seven." And he said to them, "Do you not yet understand?"

And they came to Beth-sa'ida. And some people brought to him a blind man, and begged him to touch him. And he took the blind man by the hand, and led him out of the village; and when he had spit on his eyes and laid his hands upon him, he asked him, "Do you see anything?" And he looked up and said, "I see men; but

The metal door of the Church of the Annunciation in modern Nazareth shows scenes from Jesus' life.

they look like trees, walking." Then again he laid his hands upon his eyes; and he looked intently and was restored, and saw everything clearly. And he sent him away to his home, saying, "Do not even enter the village."

And Jesus went on with his disciples, to the villages of Caesare'a Philippi; and on the way he asked his disciples, "Who do men say that I am?" And they told him, "John the Baptist; and others say, Eli'jah; and others one of the prophets." And he asked them, "But who do you say that I am?" Peter answered him, "You are the Christ." And he charged them to tell no one about him.

B. Mark 8:31–16:20

And he began to teach them that the Son of man must suffer many things, and be rejected by the elders and the chief priests and the scribes, and be killed, and after three days rise again. And he said this plainly. And Peter took him, and began to rebuke him. But turning and seeing his disciples, he rebuked Peter, and said, "Get behind me, Satan! For you are not on the side of God, but of men."

And he called to him the multitude with his disciples, and said to them, "If any man would come after me, let him deny himself and take up his cross and follow me. For whoever would save his life will lose it; and whoever loses his life for my sake and the gospel's will save it. For what does it profit a man, to gain the whole world and forfeit his life? For what can a man give in return for his life? For whoever is ashamed of me and of my words in this adulterous and sinful generation, of him will the Son of man also be ashamed, when he comes in the glory of his Father with the holy angels."

9 And he said to them, "Truly, I say to you, there are some standing here who will not taste death before they see that the kingdom of God has come with power."

And after six days Jesus took with him Peter and James and John, and led them up a high mountain apart by themselves; and he was transfigured before them, and his garments became glistening, intensely white, as no fuller on earth could bleach them. And there appeared to them Eli'jah with Moses; and they were talking to Jesus. And Peter said to Jesus, "Master, it is well that we are here; let us make three booths, one for you and one for Moses and one for Eli'jah." For he did not know what to say, for they were exceedingly afraid. And a cloud overshadowed them, and a voice came out of the cloud, "This is my beloved Son; listen to him." And suddenly looking around they no longer saw any one with them but Jesus only.

And as they were coming down the mountain, he charged them to tell no one what they had seen, until the Son of man should have risen from the dead. So they kept the matter to themselves, questioning what the rising from the dead meant. And they asked him, "Why do the scribes say that first Eli'jah must come?" And he said to them, "Eli'jah does come first to restore all things; and how is it written of the Son of man, that he should suffer many things and be treated with contempt? But I tell you that Eli'jah has come, and they did to him whatever they pleased, as it is written of him."

And when they came to the disciples, they saw a great crowd about them, and scribes arguing with them. And immediately all the crowd, when they saw him, were greatly amazed, and ran up to him and greeted him. And he asked them, "What are you discussing with them?" And one of the crowd answered him, "Teacher, I brought my son to you, for he has a dumb spirit; and wherever it seizes him, it dashes him down; and he foams and grinds his teeth and becomes rigid; and I asked your disciples to cast it out, and they were not able." And he answered them, "O faithless generation, how long am I to be with you? Bring him to me." And they brought the boy to him; and when the spirit saw him, immediately it convulsed the boy, and he fell on the ground and rolled about, foaming at the mouth. And Jesus asked his father, "How long has he had this?" And he said, "From childhood. And it has often cast him into the fire and into the water, to destroy him; but if you can do anything, have pity on us and help us." And Jesus said to him, "If you can! All things are possible to him who believes." Immediately the father of the child cried out and said, "I believe; help my unbelief!" And when Jesus saw that a crowd came running together, he rebuked the unclean spirit, saying to it, "You dumb and deaf spirit, I command you, come out of him, and never enter him again." And after crying out and convulsing him terribly, it came out, and the boy was like a corpse; so that most of them said, "He is dead." But Jesus took him by the hand and lifted him up, and he arose. And when he had entered the house, his disciples asked him privately, "Why could we not cast it out?" And he said to them, "This kind cannot be driven out by anything but prayer."

They went on from there and passed through Galilee. And he would not have any one know it; for he was teaching his disciples, saying to them, "The Son of man will be delivered into the hands of men, and they will kill him; and when he is killed, after three days he will rise." But they did not understand the saying, and they were afraid to ask him.

And they came to Caper′na-um; and when he was in the house he asked them, "What were you discussing on the way?" But they were silent; for on the way they had discussed with one another who was the greatest. And he sat down and called the twelve; and he said to them, "If any one would be first, he must be last of all and servant of all." And he took a child, and put him in the midst of them; and taking him in his arms, he said to them, "Whoever receives one such child in my name receives me; and whoever receives me, receives not me but him who sent me."

John said to him, "Teacher, we saw a man casting out demons in your name, and we forbade him, because he was not following us." But Jesus said, "Do not forbid him; for no one who does a mighty work in my name will be able soon after to speak evil of me. For he that is not against us is for us. For truly, I say to you, whoever gives you a cup of water to drink because you bear the name of Christ, will by no means lose his reward.

"Whoever causes one of these little ones who believe in me to sin, it would be better for him if a great millstone were hung around his neck and he were thrown into the sea. And if your hand causes you to sin, cut it off; it is better for you to enter life maimed than with two hands to go to hell, to the unquenchable fire. And if your foot causes you to sin, cut it off; it is better for you to enter life lame than with two feet to be thrown into hell. And if your eye causes you to sin, pluck it out; it is better for you to enter the kingdom of God with one eye than with two eyes to be thrown into hell, where their worm does not die, and the fire is not quenched. For every one will be salted with fire. Salt is good; but if the salt has lost its saltness, how will you season it? Have salt in yourselves, and be at peace with one another."

10 And he left there and went to the region of Judea and beyond the Jordan, and crowds gathered to him again; and again, as his custom was, he taught them.

And Pharisees came up and in order to test him asked, "Is it lawful for a man to divorce his wife?" He answered them. "What did Moses command you?" They said, "Moses allowed a man to write a certificate of divorce, and to put her away." But Jesus said to them, "For your hardness of heart he wrote you his commandment. But from the beginning of creation, 'God made them male and female.' 'For this reason a man shall leave his father and mother and be joined to his wife, and the two shall become one flesh.' So they are no longer two but one flesh. What therefore God has joined together, let not man put asunder."

And in the house the disciples asked him again about this matter. And he said to them, "Whoever divorces his wife and marries another, commits adultery against her; and if she divorces her husband and marries another, she commits adultery."

And they were bringing children to him, that he might touch them; and the disciples rebuked them. But when Jesus saw it he was indignant, and said to them, "Let the children come to me, do not hinder them; for to such belongs the kingdom of God. Truly, I say to you, whoever does not receive the kingdom of God like a child shall not enter it." And he took them in his arms and blessed them, laying his hands upon them.

And as he was setting out on his journey, a man ran up and knelt before him, and asked him, "Good Teacher, what must I do to inherit eternal life?" And Jesus said to him, "Why do you call me good? No one is good but God alone. You know the commandments: 'Do not kill, Do not commit adultery, Do not steal, Do not bear false witness, Do not defraud, Honor your father and mother.'" And he said to him, "Teacher, all these I have observed from my youth." And Jesus looking upon him loved him, and said to him, "You lack one thing; go, sell what you have, and give to the poor, and you will have treasure in heaven; and come, follow me." At that saying his countenance fell, and he went away sorrowful; for he had great possessions.

And Jesus looked around and said to his disciples, "How hard it will be for those who have riches to enter the kingdom of God!" And the disciples were amazed at his words. But Jesus said to them again, "Children, how hard it is to enter the kingdom of God! It is easier for a camel to go through the eye of a needle than for a rich man to enter the kingdom of God." And they were exceedingly astonished, and said to him, "Then who can be saved?" Jesus looked at them and said, "With men it is impossible, but not with God; for all things are possible with God." Peter began to say to him, "Lo, we have left everything and followed you." Jesus said,

"Truly, I say to you, there is no one who has left house or brothers or sisters or mother or father or children or lands, for my sake and for the gospel, who will not receive a hundredfold now in this time, houses and brothers and sisters and mothers and children and lands, with persecutions, and in the age to come eternal life. But many that are first will be last, and the last first."

And they were on the road, going up to Jerusalem, and Jesus was walking ahead of them; and they were amazed, and those who followed were afraid. And taking the twelve again, he began to tell them what was to happen to him, saying, "Behold, we are going up to Jerusalem; and the Son of man will be delivered to the chief priests and the scribes, and they will condemn him to death, and deliver him to the Gentiles; and they will mock him, and spit upon him, and scourge him, and kill him; and after three days he will rise."

And James and John, the sons of Zeb'edee, came forward to him, and said to him, "Teacher, we want you to do for us whatever we ask of you." And he said to them, "What do you want me to do for you?" And they said to him, "Grant us to sit, one at your right hand and one at your left, in your glory." But Jesus said to them, "You do not know what you are asking. Are you able to drink the cup that I drink, or to be baptized with the baptism with which I am baptized?" And they said to him, "We are able." And Jesus said to them, "The cup that I drink you will drink; and with the baptism with which I am baptized, you will be baptized; but to sit at my right hand or at my left is not mine to grant, but it is for those for whom it has been prepared." And when the ten heard it, they began to be indignant at James and John. And Jesus called them to him and said to them, "You know that those who are supposed to rule over the Gentiles lord it over them, and their great men exercise authority over them. But it shall not be so among you; but whoever would be great among you must be your servant, and whoever would be first among you must be slave of all. For the Son of man also came not to be served but to serve, and to give his life as a ransom for many."

And they came to Jericho; and as he was leaving Jericho with his disciples and a great multitude, Bartimae'us, a blind beggar, the son of Timae'us, was sitting by the roadside. And when he heard that it was Jesus of Nazareth, he began to cry out and say, "Jesus, Son of David, have mercy on me!" And many rebuked him, telling him to be silent; but he cried out all the more, "Son of

David, have mercy on me!" And Jesus stopped and said, "Call him." And they called the blind man, saying to him, "Take heart; rise, he is calling you." And throwing off his mantle he sprang up and came to Jesus. And Jesus said to him, "What do you want me to do for you?" And the blind man said to him, "Master, let me receive my sight." And Jesus said to him, "Go your way; your faith has made you well." And immediately he received his sight and followed him on the way.

11 And when they drew near to Jerusalem, to Beth'phage and Bethany, at the Mount of Olives, he sent two of his disciples, and said to them, "Go into the village opposite you, and immediately as you enter it you will find a colt tied, on which no one has ever sat; untie it and bring it. If any one says to you, 'Why are you doing this?' say, 'The Lord has need of it and will send it back here immediately.'" And they went away, and found a colt tied at the door out in the open street; and they untied it. And those who stood there said to them, "What are you doing, untying the colt?" And they told them what Jesus had said; and they let them go. And they brought the colt to Jesus, and threw their garments on it; and he sat upon it. And many spread their garments on the road, and others spread leafy branches which they had cut from the fields. And those who went before and those who followed cried out, "Hosanna! Blessed is he who comes in the name of the Lord! Blessed is the kingdom of our father David that is coming! Hosanna in the highest!"

And he entered Jerusalem, and went into the temple; and when he had looked round at everything, as it was already late, he went out to Bethany with the twelve.

On the following day, when they came from Bethany, he was hungry. And seeing in the distance a fig tree in leaf, he went to see if he could find anything on it. When he came to it, he found nothing but leaves, for it was not the season for figs. And he said to it, "May no one ever eat fruit from you again." And his disciples heard it.

And they came to Jerusalem. And he entered the temple and began to drive out those who sold and those who bought in the temple, and he overturned the tables of the money-changers and the seats of those who sold pigeons; and he would not allow any one to carry anything through the temple. And he taught, and said to them, "Is it not written, 'My house shall be called a house of

A fig tree.

prayer for all the nations'? But you have made it a den of robbers." And the chief priests and the scribes heard it and sought a way to destroy him; for they feared him, because all the multitude was astonished at his teaching. And when evening came they went out of the city.

As they passed by in the morning, they saw the fig tree withered away to its roots. And Peter remembered and said to him, "Master, look! The fig tree which you cursed has withered." And Jesus answered them, "Have faith in God. Truly, I say to you, whoever says to this mountain, 'Be taken up and cast into the sea,' and does not doubt in his heart, but believes that what he says will come to pass, it will be done for him. Therefore I tell you, whatever you ask in prayer, believe that you have received it, and it will be yours. And whenever you stand praying, forgive, if you have anything against any one; so that your Father also who is in heaven may forgive you your trespasses."

And they came again to Jerusalem. And as he was walking in the temple, the chief priests and the scribes and the elders came to him, and they said to him, "By what authority are you doing these things, or who gave you this authority to do them?" Jesus said to them, "I will ask you a question; answer me, and I will tell you by what authority I do these things. Was the baptism of John from heaven or from men? Answer me." And they argued with one another, "If we say, 'From heaven,' he will say, 'Why then did you not believe him?' But shall we say, 'From men'?"—they were afraid of the people, for all held that John was a real prophet. So they answered Jesus, "We do not know." And Jesus said to them, "Neither will I tell you by what authority I do these things."

12 And he began to speak to them in parables. "A man planted a vineyard, and set a hedge around it, and dug a pit for the wine press, and built a tower, and let it out to tenants, and went into another country. When the time came, he sent a servant to the tenants, to get from them some of the fruit of the vineyard. And they took him and beat him, and sent him away empty-handed. Again he sent to them another servant, and they wounded him in the head, and treated him shamefully. And he sent another, and him they killed; and so with many others, some they beat and some they killed. He had still one other, a beloved son; finally he sent him to them, saying, 'They will respect my son.' But those tenants said to one another, 'This is the heir; come, let us kill him, and the inheritance will be ours.' And they took him and killed him, and cast him out of the vineyard. What will the owner of the vineyard do? He will come and destroy the tenants, and give the vineyard to others. Have you not read this scripture:

'The very stone which the builders rejected
has become the head of the corner;
this was the Lord's doing,
and it is marvelous in our eyes'?"

And they tried to arrest him, but feared the multitude, for they perceived that he had told the parable against them; so they left him and went away.

And they sent to him some of the Pharisees and some of the Hero'di-ans, to entrap him in his talk. And they came and said to him, "Teacher, we know that you are true, and care for no man; for you do not regard the position of men, but truly teach the way of God. Is it lawful to pay taxes to Caesar, or not? Should we pay them, or should we not?" But knowing their hypocrisy, he said to them, "Why put me to the test? Bring me a coin, and let me look at it." And they brought one. And he said to them, "Whose likeness and inscription is this?" They said to him, "Caesar's." Jesus said to them, "Render to Caesar the things that are Caesar's, and to God the things that are God's." And they were amazed at him.

And Sad'ducees came to him, who say that there is no resurrection; and they asked him a question, saying, "Teacher, Moses wrote for us that if a man's brother dies and leaves a wife, but leaves no child, the man must take the wife, and raise up children for his brother. There were seven brothers; the first took a wife, and when he died left no children; and the second took her, and died, leaving no children; and the third likewise; and the seven left no children. Last of all the woman also died. In the resurrection whose wife will she be? For the seven had her as wife."

Jesus said to them, "Is not this why you are wrong, that you know neither the scriptures nor the power of God? For when they rise from the dead, they neither marry nor are given in marriage, but are like angels in heaven. And as for the dead being raised, have you not read in the book of Moses, in the passage about the bush, how God said to him, 'I am the God of Abraham, and the God of Isaac, and the God of Jacob'? He is not God of the dead, but of the living; you are quite wrong."

And one of the scribes came up and heard them disputing with one another, and seeing that he answered them well, asked him, "Which commandment is the first of all?" Jesus answered, "The first is, 'Hear, O Israel: The Lord our God, the Lord is one; and you shall love the Lord your God with all your heart, and with all your soul, and with all your mind, and with all your strength.' The second is this, 'You shall love your neighbor as yourself.' There is no other commandment greater than these." And the scribe said to him, "You are right, Teacher; you have truly said that he is one, and there is no other but he; and to love him with all the heart, and with all the understanding, and with all the strength, and to love one's neighbor as oneself, is much more than all whole burnt offerings and sacrifices." And when Jesus saw that he answered wisely, he said to him, "You are not far from the kingdom of God." And after that no one dared to ask him any question.

And as Jesus taught in the temple, he said, "How can the scribes say that the Christ is the son of David? David himself, inspired by the Holy Spirit, declared,

'The Lord said to my Lord,

Sit at my right hand, till I put thy enemies under thy feet.'

David himself calls him Lord; so how is he his son?" And the great throng heard him gladly.

And in his teaching he said, "Beware of the scribes, who like to go about in long robes, and to have salutations in the market places and the best seats in the synagogues and the places of honor at feasts, who devour widow's houses and for a pretense make long prayers. They will receive the greater condemnation."

And he sat down opposite the treasury, and watched the multitude putting money into the treasury. Many rich people put in large sums. And a poor widow came, and put in two copper coins, which make a penny. And he called his disciples to him, and said to them, "Truly, I say to you, this poor widow has put in more than all those who are contributing to the treasury. For they all contributed out of their abundance; but she out of her poverty has put in everything she had, her whole living."

13 And as he came out of the temple, one of his disciples said to him, "Look, Teacher, what wonderful stones and what wonderful buildings!" And Jesus said to him, "Do you see these great buildings? There will not be left here one stone upon another, that will not be thrown down."

And as he sat on the Mount of Olives opposite the temple, Peter and James and John and Andrew asked him privately, "Tell us, when will this be, and what will be the sign when these things are all to be accomplished?" And Jesus began to say to them, "Take heed that no one leads you astray. Many will come in my name, saying, 'I am he!' and they will lead many astray. And when you hear of wars and rumors of wars, do not be alarmed; this must take place, but the end is not yet. For nation will rise against nation, and kingdom against kingdom; there will be earthquakes in various places, there will be famines; this is but the beginning of the birth-pangs.

"But take heed to yourselves; for they will deliver you up to councils; and you will be beaten in synagogues; and you will stand before governors and kings for my sake, to bear testimony before them. And the gospel must first be preached to all nations. And when they bring you to trial and deliver you up, do not be anxious beforehand what you are to say; but say whatever is given you in that hour, for it is not you who speak, but the Holy Spirit. And brother will deliver up brother to death, and the father his child, and children will rise against parents and have them put to death; and you will be hated by all for my name's sake. But he who endures to the end will be saved.

"But when you see the desolating sacrilege set up where it ought not to be (let the reader understand), then let those who are in Judea flee to the mountains; let him who is on the housetop not go down, nor enter his house, to take anything away; and let him who is in the field not turn back to take his mantle. And alas for those who are with child and for those who give suck in those days! Pray that it may not happen in winter. For in those days there will be such tribulation as has not been from the beginning of the creation which God created until now, and never will be. And if the Lord had not shortened the days, no human being would be saved; but for the sake of the elect, whom he chose, he shortened the days. And then if any one says to you, 'Look, here is the Christ!' or 'Look, there he is!' do not believe it. False Christs and false prophets will arise and show signs and wonders, to lead astray, if possible, the elect. But take heed; I have told you all things beforehand.

"But in those days, after that tribulation, the sun will be darkened, and the moon will not give its light, and the stars will be falling from heaven, and the powers in the heavens will be shaken.

And then they will see the Son of man coming in clouds with great power and glory. And then he will send out the angels, and gather his elect from the four winds, from the ends of the earth to the ends of heaven.

"From the fig tree learn its lesson: as soon as its branch becomes tender and puts forth its leaves, you know that summer is near. So also, when you see these things taking place, you know that he is near, at the very gates. Truly, I say to you, this generation will not pass away before all these things take place. Heaven and earth will pass away, but my words will not pass away.

"But of that day or that hour no one knows, not even the angels in heaven, nor the Son, but only the Father. Take heed, watch; for you do not know when the time will come. It is like a man going on a journey, when he leaves home and puts his servants in charge, each with his work, and commands the doorkeeper to be on the watch. Watch therefore—for you do not know when the master of the house will come, in the evening, or at midnight, or at cock-crow, or in the morning—lest he come suddenly and find you asleep. And what I say to you I say to all: Watch."

14 It was now two days before the Passover and the feast of Unleavened Bread. And the chief priests and the scribes were seeking how to arrest him by stealth, and kill him; for they said, "Not during the feast, lest there be a tumult of the people."

And while he was at Bethany in the house of Simon the leper, as he sat at table, a woman came with an alabaster flask of ointment of pure nard, very costly, and she broke the flask and poured it over his head. But there were some who said to themselves indignantly, "Why was this ointment thus wasted? For this ointment might have been sold for more than three hundred denarii, and given to the poor." And they reproached her. But Jesus said, "Let her alone; why do you trouble her? She has done a beautiful thing to me. For you always have the poor with you, and whenever you will, you can do good to them; but you will not always have me. She has done what she could; she has anointed my body beforehand for burying. And truly, I say to you, wherever the gospel is preached in the whole world, what she has done will be told in memory of her."

Then Judas Iscariot, who was one of the twelve, went to the chief priests in order to betray him to them. And when they heard it they were glad, and promised to give him money. And he sought an opportunity to betray him.

And on the first day of Unleavened Bread, when they sacrificed the passover lamb, his disciples said to him, "Where will you have us go and prepare for you to eat the passover?" And he sent two of his disciples, and said to them, "Go into the city, and a man carrying a jar of water will meet you; follow him, and wherever he enters, say to the householder, 'The Teacher says, Where is my guest room, where I am to eat the passover with my disciples?' And he will show you a large upper room furnished and ready; there prepare for us." And the disciples set out and went to the city, and found it as he had told them; and they prepared the passover.

And when it was evening he came with the twelve. And as they were at table eating, Jesus said, "Truly, I say to you, one of you will betray me, one who is eating with me." They began to be sorrowful, and to say to him one after another, "Is it I?" He said to them, "It is one of the twelve, one who is dipping bread into the dish with me. For the Son of man goes as it is written of him, but woe to that man by whom the Son of man is betrayed! It would have been better for that man if he had not been born."

And as they were eating, he took bread, and blessed, and broke it, and gave it to them, and said, "Take; this is my body." And he took a cup, and when he had given thanks he gave it to them, and they all drank of it. And he said to them, "This is my blood of the covenant, which is poured out for many. Truly, I say to you, I shall not drink again of the fruit of the vine until that day when I drink it new in the kingdom of God."

And when they had sung a hymn, they went out to the Mount of Olives. And Jesus said to them, "You will all fall away; for it is written, 'I will strike the shepherd, and the sheep will be scattered.' But after I am raised up, I will go before you to Galilee." Peter said to him, "Even though they all fall away, I will not." And Jesus said to him, "Truly, I say to you, this very night, before the cock crows twice, you will deny me three times." But he said vehemently, "If I must die with you, I will not deny you." And they all said the same.

And they went to a place which was called Gethsem'ane; and he said to his disciples, "Sit here, while I pray." And he took with him Peter and James and John, and began to be greatly distressed and troubled. And he said to them, "My soul is very sorrowful, even to death; remain here, and watch." And going a little farther, he fell on the ground and prayed that, if it were possible, the hour might pass from him. And he said, "Abba, Father, all things are possible to thee; remove this cup from me; yet not what I will, but what thou wilt." And he came and found them sleeping, and he said to Peter, "Simon, are you asleep? Could you not watch one hour? Watch and pray that you may not enter into temptation; the spirit indeed is willing, but the flesh is weak." And again he went away and prayed, saying the same words. And again he came and found them sleeping, for their eyes were very heavy; and they did not know what to answer him. And he came the third time, and said to them, "Are you still sleeping and taking your rest? It is enough; the hour has come; the Son of man is betrayed into the hands of sinners. Rise, let us be going; see, my betrayer is at hand."

And immediately, while he was still speaking, Judas came, one of the twelve, and with him a crowd with swords and clubs, from the chief priests and the scribes and the elders. Now the betrayer had given them a sign, saying, "The one I shall kiss is the man; seize him and lead him away under guard." And when he came, he went up to him at once, and said, "Master!" And he kissed him. And they laid hands on him and seized him. But one of those who stood by drew his sword, and struck the slave of the high priest and cut off his ear. And Jesus said to them, "Have you come out as against a robber, with swords and clubs to capture me? Day after day I was with you in the temple teaching, and you did not seize me. But let the scriptures be fulfilled." And they all forsook him, and fled.

And a young man followed him, with nothing but a linen cloth about his body; and they seized him, but he left the linen cloth and ran away naked.

And they led Jesus to the high priest; and all the chief priests and the elders and the scribes were assembled. And Peter had followed him at a distance, right into the courtyard of the high priest; and he was sitting with the guards, and warming himself at the fire. Now the chief priests and the whole council sought testimony against Jesus to put him to death; but they found none. For many bore false witness against him, and their witness did not agree. And some stood up and bore false witness against him, saying, "We heard him say, 'I will destroy this temple that is made with hands, and in three days I will build another, not made with

A mosaic showing Judas' betrayal of Jesus.

hands.'" Yet not even so did their testimony agree. And the high priest stood up in the midst, and asked Jesus, "Have you no answer to make? What is it that these men testify against you?" But he was silent and made no answer. Again the high priest asked him, "Are you the Christ, the Son of the Blessed?" And Jesus said, "I am; and you will see the Son of man seated at the right hand of Power, and coming with the clouds of heaven." And the high priest tore his garments, and said, "Why do we still need witnesses? You have heard his blasphemy. What is your decision?" And they all condemned him as deserving death. And some began to spit on him, and to cover his face, and to strike him, saying to him, "Prophesy!" And the guards received him with blows.

And as Peter was below in the courtyard, one of the maids of the high priest came; and seeing Peter warming himself, she looked at him, and said, "You also were with the Nazarene, Jesus." But he denied it, saying, "I neither know nor understand what you mean." And he went out into the gateway. And the maid saw him, and began again to say to the bystanders, "This man is one of them." But again he denied it. And after a little while again the bystanders said to Peter, "Certainly you are one of them; for you are a Galilean." But he began to invoke a curse on himself and to swear, "I do not know this man of whom you speak." And immediately the cock crowed a second time. And Peter remembered how Jesus had said to him, "Before the cock crows twice, you will deny me three times." And he broke down and wept.

15 And as soon as it was morning the chief priests, with the elders and scribes, and the whole council held a consultation; and they bound Jesus and led him away and delivered him to Pilate. And Pilate asked him, "Are you the King of the Jews?" And he answered him, "You have said so." And the chief priests accused him of many things. And Pilate again asked him, "Have you no answer to make? See how many charges they bring against you." But Jesus made no further answer, so that Pilate wondered.

Now at the feast he used to release for them one prisoner for whom they asked. And among the rebels in prison, who had committed murder in the insurrection, there was a man called Barab'bas. And the crowd came up and began to ask Pilate to do as he was wont to do for them. And he answered them, "Do you want me to release for you the King of the Jews?" For he perceived that it was out of envy that the chief priests had delivered him up. But the chief priests stirred up the crowd to have him release for them Barab'bas instead. And Pilate again said to them, "Then what shall I do with the man whom you call the King of the Jews?" And they cried out again, "Crucify him." And Pilate said to them, "Why, what evil has he done?" But they shouted all the more, "Crucify him." So Pilate, wishing to satisfy the crowd, released for them Barab'bas; and having scourged Jesus, he delivered him to be crucified.

And the soldiers led him away inside the palace (that is, the praetorium); and they called together the whole battalion. And they clothed him in a purple cloak, and plaiting a crown of thorns they put it on him. And they began to salute him, "Hail, King of the Jews!" And they struck his head with a reed, and spat upon him, and they knelt down in homage to him. And when they had mocked him, they stripped him of the purple cloak, and put his own clothes on him. And they led him out to crucify him.

And they compelled a passer-by, Simon of Cyre'ne, who was coming in from the country, the father of Alexander and Rufus, to carry his cross. And they brought him to the place called Gol'gotha (which means the place of a skull). And they offered him wine mingled with myrrh; but he did not take it. And they crucified him, and divided his garments among them, casting lots for them, to decide what each should take. And it was the third hour, when they crucified him. And the inscription of the charge against him read, "The King of the Jews." And with him they crucified two robbers, one on his right and one on his left. And those who passed by derided him, wagging their heads, and saying, "Aha! You who would destroy the temple and build it in three days, save yourself, and come down from the cross!" So also the chief priests mocked him to one another with the scribes, saying, "He saved others; he cannot save himself. Let the Christ, the King of Israel, come down now from the cross, that we may see and believe." Those who were crucified with him also reviled him.

And when the sixth hour had come, there was darkness over the whole land until the ninth hour. And at the ninth hour Jesus cried with a loud voice, "E'lo-i, E'lo-i, la'ma sabachtha'ni?" which means, "My God, my God, why hast thou forsaken me?" And some of the bystanders hearing it said, "Behold, he is calling Eli'jah." And one ran and, filling a sponge full of vinegar, put it on a reed and gave it to him to drink, saying, "Wait, let us see whether Eli'jah will come to take him down." And Jesus uttered a loud cry, and breathed his last. And the curtain of the temple was torn in two, from top to bottom. And when the centurion, who stood facing him, saw that he thus breathed his last, he said, "Truly this man was the Son of God!"

There were also women looking on from afar, among whom were Mary Mag'dalene, and Mary the mother of James the younger and of Joses, and Salo'me, who, when he was in Galilee, followed him, and ministered to him; and also many other women who came up with him to Jerusalem.

And when evening had come, since it was the day of Preparation, that is, the day before the sabbath, Joseph of Arimathe'a, a respected member of the council, who was also himself looking for the kingdom of God, took courage and went to Pilate, and asked for the body of Jesus. And Pilate wondered if he were already dead; and summoning the centurion, he asked him whether he was already dead. And when he learned from the centurion that he was dead, he granted the body to Joseph. And he bought a linen shroud, and taking him down, wrapped him in the linen shroud, and laid him in a tomb which had been hewn out of the rock; and he rolled a stone against the door of the tomb. Mary Mag'dalene and Mary the mother of Joses saw where he was laid.

16 And when the sabbath was past, Mary Mag'dalene, and Mary the mother of James, and Salo'me, bought spices, so that they might go and anoint him. And very early on the first day of the week they went to the tomb when the sun had risen. And they were saying to one another, "Who will roll away the stone for us from the door of the tomb?" And looking up, they saw that the stone was rolled back—it was very large. And entering the tomb, they saw a young man sitting on the right side, dressed in a white robe; and they were amazed. And he said to them, "Do not be amazed; you seek Jesus of Nazareth, who was crucified. He has risen, he is not here; see the place were they laid him. But go, tell his disciples and Peter that he is going before you to Galilee; there you will see him, as he told you." And they went out and fled from the tomb; for trembling and astonishment had come upon them; and they said nothing to any one, for they were afraid.

Now when he rose early on the first day of the week, he appeared first to Mary Magdalene, from whom he had cast out

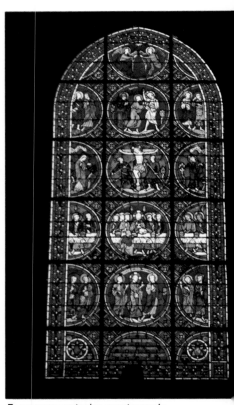

For many centuries most people could not read, and the stories of the Bible were communicated to them in sculpture, painting, and stained-glass windows. This medieval window shows Jesus' entry into Jerusalem, the Last Supper, the Crucifixion, and the Resurrection.

seven demons. She went out and told those who had been with him, and they mourned and wept. But when they heard that he was alive and had been seen by her, they would not believe it.

After this he appeared in another form to two of them, as they were walking into the country. And they went back and told the rest, but they did not believe them.

Afterward he appeared to the eleven themselves as they sat at table; and he upbraided them for their unbelief and hardness of heart, because they had not believed those who saw him after he had risen. And he said to them, "Go into all the world and preach the gospel to the whole creation. He who believes and is baptized will be saved; but he who does not believe will be condemned. And these signs will accompany those who believe: in my name they will cast out demons; they will speak in new tongues; they will pick up serpents, and if they drink any deadly thing, it will not hurt them; they will lay their hands on the sick, and they will recover."

So then the Lord Jesus, after he had spoken to them, was taken up into heaven, and sat down at the right hand of God. And they went forth and preached everywhere, while the Lord worked with them and confirmed the message by the signs that attended it. Amen.

Today, as in biblical times, the good shepherd carefully watches his flock.

READING 12

He Lived the Good Life*

A. The Gathering of Disciples

As he walked along the shore
As he wandered by the sea
He saw two brothers casting nets
And he hollered "Follow me."
And then going on from there
Long the shore of Galilee
He saw two brothers mendin' nets
And he told them "Follow me."
Follow me Peter
Follow me Andrew
Follow me James and John
Follow me Follow me
That's what he said, and they continued on.
There was Matthew, there was Tom.
There was Judas who was wrong
But when he said "Come follow me"
They dropped their work and came along.
And to the people on the hill
He continued with his plea
To the poor and to the rich

*From the record *He Lived the Good Life* by Richard Wilson (Minneapolis: Wil-Song, Inc., 1973).

He kept saying "Follow me,"
Follow me sinner, Follow me brother
Follow me friend and foe.
Follow me Follow me Follow me,
We've got places to go.
To the multitudes and crowds
To the child on his knee
To the woman by the well
Come my friends and follow me,
Come my friends and follow me,
Come my friends and follow me.

B. The Parables

Storyteller, yes he was the storytellin' kind
He painted pictures in their mind,
It was the way he let them see
How things were really s'posed to be.
He told a parable about the mustard seed
And how it grows so very tall
But when it starts out
That tiny mustard seed is very small.
He told a parable about the seeds of wheat
And how they spring to life within the soil
But if they're sown on rocks
Or on the barren land
Those seeds will spoil.
Storyteller, yes he was the storytellin' kind
He painted pictures in their mind
It was the way he let them see
How things were really s'posed to be
He told a parable about the shepherd man
And when he found the lamb he was so glad
He told a parable about the prodigal who left his dad.
He used the wine, he used the bread, he used the fish,
He used the sea,
He used the pearls and kings and birds and rings
To help him tell his story.

This Galilean farmer separates wheat from chaff in exactly the same way as did the farmers to whom Jesus spoke in Galilee.

He told a parable about a friendly man
A good Samaritan
Who really cared.
He told a parable about a wealthy man
Who never shared.
He told a parable about a Pharisee
Who prayed he'd never be like other men.
He told the parables to keep the people all away from sin.
Storyteller, yes he was the storytellin' kind
He painted pictures in their mind
It was the way he let them see
How things were really s'posed to be.

READING 13

Amazing Grace*

Amazing grace! how sweet the sound
That saved a wretch like me!
I once was lost, but now am found,
Was blind, but now I see.

'Twas grace that taught my heart to fear,
And grace my fears relieved;
How precious did that grace appear
The hour I first believed.

Through many dangers, toils and snares,
I have already come;
'Tis grace hath brought me safe thus far,
And grace will lead me home.

When we've been there ten thousand years,
Bright shining as the sun,
We've no less days to sing God's praise
Than when we first begun.
Amen.

*From the *Baptist Standard Hymnal* (Nashville, Tenn.: Sunday School Publishing Board, National Baptist Convention, U.S.A., 1973), p. 427.

A representation of the Crucifixion in a French window.
The letters INRI *are Latin for* Iesus Nazarenus Rex Iudaeorum *("Jesus of Nazareth, King of the Jews").*

READING 14

Salvation

A. Matthew 1:20–22*

But as he considered this, behold, an angel of the Lord appeared to him in a dream, saying, "Joseph, son of David, do not fear to take Mary your wife, for that which is conceived in her is of the Holy Spirit; she will bear a son, and you shall call his name Jesus, for he will save his people from their sins." All this took place to fulfill what the Lord had spoken by the prophet.

B. Hebrews 2:9

But we see Jesus, who for a little while was made lower than the angels, crowned with glory and honor because of the suffering of death, so that by the grace of God he might taste death for every one.

C. John 3:16–18 (Atonement)

For God so loved the world that he gave his only Son, that whoever believes in him should not perish but have eternal life. For God sent the Son into the world, not to condemn the world, but that the world might be saved through him. He who believes in him is not condemned; he who does not believe is condemned already, because he has not believed in the name of the only Son of God.

*This and the following passages are from *The Common Bible*, Revised Standard Version.

The Crucifixion has been a
central theme in Christian art.

READING 15
Grace

A. Titus 2:11–14*

For the grace of God has appeared for the salvation of all men, training us to renounce irreligion and worldly passions, and to live sober, upright, and godly lives in this world, awaiting our blessed hope, the appearing of the glory of our great God and Savior Jesus Christ, who gave himself for us to redeem us from all iniquity and to purify for himself a people of his own who are zealous for good deeds.

B. Romans 5:18–21

Then as one man's trespass led to condemnation for all men, so one man's act of righteousness leads to acquittal and life for all men. For as by one man's disobedience many were made sinners, so by one man's obedience many will be made righteous. Law came in, to increase the trespass; but where sin increased, grace abounded all the more, so that, as sin reigned in death, grace also might reign through righteousness to eternal life through Jesus Christ our Lord.

*Ibid.

C. 1 Corinthians 1:3

Grace to you and peace from God our Father and the Lord Jesus Christ.

D. Ephesians 3:1–10

For this reason I, Paul, a prisoner for Christ Jesus on behalf of you Gentiles—assuming that you have heard of the stewardship of God's grace that was given to me for you, how the mystery was made known to me by revelation, as I have written briefly. When you read this you can perceive my insight into the mystery of Christ, which was not made known to the sons of men in other generations as it has now been revealed to his holy apostles and prophets by the Spirit; that is, how the Gentiles are fellow heirs, members of the same body, and partakers of the promise in Christ Jesus through the gospel.

Of this gospel I was made a minister according to the gift of God's grace which was given me by the working of his power. To me, though I am the very least of all the saints, this grace was given, to preach to the Gentiles the unsearchable riches of Christ, and to make all men see what is the plan of the mystery hidden for ages in God who created all things; that through the church the manifold wisdom of God might now be made known to the principalities and powers in the heavenly places.

READING 16

Incarnate

A. Council of Chalcedon, 451*

The top panel in this Swiss stained-glass window depicts the Father (hand), Son (cross), and Holy Spirit (dove). Jesus, Mary, and Joseph are shown in the center panel. A chalice, prayerbook, saw, and ring appear in the bottom panel.

Therefore, following the holy Fathers, we all with one accord teach men to acknowledge one and the same Son, our Lord Jesus Christ, at once complete in Godhead and complete in manhood, truly God and truly man, consisting also of a reasonable soul and body; of one substance with the Father as regards his Godhead, and at the same time of one substance with us as regards his manhood; like us in all respects, apart from sin; as regards his Godhead, begotten of the Father before the ages, but yet as regards his manhood begotten, for us men and for our salvation, of Mary the Virgin, the God-bearer; one and the same Christ, Son, Lord, Only-begotten, recognized in two natures, without confusion, without change, without division, without separation; the distinction of natures being in no way annulled by the union, but rather the characteristics of each nature being preserved and coming together to form one person and subsistence, not as parted or separated into two persons, but one and the same Son and Only-begotten God the Word, Lord Jesus Christ; even as the prophets from earliest times spoke of him, and our Lord Jesus Christ himself taught us, and the creed of the Fathers has handed down to us.

*From Henry Bettenson, ed., *Documents of the Christian Church*, 2d ed. (New York: Oxford University Press, 1963), pp. 51–52.

B. John 1:14*

And the Word became flesh and dwelt among us, full of grace and truth; we have beheld his glory, glory as of the only Son from the Father.

C. 1 Timothy 2:5–6

For there is one God, and there is one mediator between God and men, the man Christ Jesus, who gave himself as a ransom for all, the testimony to which was borne at the proper time.

D. Hebrews 2:14–15

Since therefore the children share in flesh and blood, he himself likewise partook of the same nature, that through death he might destroy him who has the power of death, that is, the devil, and deliver all those who through fear of death were subject to lifelong bondage.

*This and the following passages are from *The Common Bible,* Revised Standard Version.

READING 17

Resurrection

A. The Resurrection*

Did you hear the good news, did you hear
   that he's not there no more?
Did you hear the good news, did you hear
   that they rolled away the door?
Did you hear that he's livin' again?
Did you hear he's back, fishin' for men?
If you haven't heard, then I'm passin' the word,
   that he's livin' again.

Did you hear the good news, did you hear that
   he's walkin' around?
Did you hear the good news, did you know that
   it's life that he's found?
Did you hear that he's livin' again?
Did you hear he's back, fishin' for men?
If you haven't heard, then I'm passin' the word,
   that he's livin' again.

There he was along the shore
Watchin' us fish in Galilee.
It was there we heard his voice once more,
Hollerin' out "Follow me."

*From the record *He Lived the Good Life* by Richard Wilson (Minneapolis: Wil-Song, Inc., 1973).

Follow me sinner
Follow me brother
Follow me friend and foe.
Follow me
Follow me
Follow me
We've got places to go.
Did you hear the good news, even Thomas says that it's true.
That he's up and alive
He did just what he said he would do.
Did you hear that he's livin' again?
Did you hear he's back, fishin' for men?
If you haven't heard, then I'm passin' the word,
  That he's livin' again.

B. 1 Corinthians 15:12–19*

Now if Christ is preached as raised from the dead, how can some of you say that there is no resurrection of the dead? But if there is no resurrection of the dead, then Christ has not been raised; if Christ has not been raised, then our preaching is in vain and your faith is in vain. We are even found to be misrepresenting God, because we testified of God that he raised Christ, whom he did not raise if it is true that the dead are not raised. For if the dead are not raised, then Christ has not been raised. If Christ has not been raised, your faith is futile and you are still in your sins. Then those also who have fallen asleep in Christ have perished. If for this life only we have hoped in Christ, we are of all men most to be pitied.

*From *The Common Bible*, Revised Standard Version.

READING 18

The Rapture

1 Thessalonians 4:13–18*

But we would not have you ignorant, brethren, concerning those who are asleep, that you may not grieve as others do who have no hope. For since we believe that Jesus died and rose again, even so, through Jesus, God will bring with him those who have fallen asleep. For this we declare to you by the word of the Lord, that we who are alive, who are left until the coming of the Lord, shall not precede those who have fallen asleep. For the Lord himself will descend from heaven with a cry of command, with the arch-angel's call, and with the sound of the trumpet of God. And the dead in Christ will rise first; then we who are alive, who are left, shall be caught up together with them in the clouds to meet the Lord in the air; and so we shall always be with the Lord. Therefore comfort one another with these words.

Entrance to the garden tomb of Jesus.

*Ibid.

The dove, a well-known symbol for the Holy Spirit.

READING 19

The Holy Spirit

A. The Pentecost Event*

After the death and resurrection of Jesus, while the religious authorities of Jerusalem believed that Jesus was out of the way for good, something happened to the Apostles which transformed them and changed everything for them. This event took place fifty days after Easter, at the time of the celebration of Pentecost.

. . . Jesus often chided [the Apostles] for their inability to understand or believe what he told them. It was often necessary for Jesus to explain his teachings in detail in order to overcome the way the disciples misunderstood things.

As the antagonism of the religious leaders of the times builds against Jesus, his disciples become more and more fearful for their lives. They keep pressing Jesus to restore the ancient kingdom of David, which they believed was the sense of the promises made through the prophets.

But their dreams are shattered when Jesus is arrested and condemned to death. Peter, the accepted leader among the twelve, denies even knowing Jesus for fear of being arrested himself. After Jesus rises from the dead, he shows himself to the disciples, he talks with them, he even eats with them. But the

*From Rev. K. J. MacDonald, *Celebrate the Spirit As Gift* (Winnipeg, Manitoba, Canada: Winnipeg Catholic Pastoral Centre, 1973), pp. 28–29.

disciples lock themselves in a room, afraid to go out because they might be arrested as followers of Jesus.

This could have been the end. Had this situation not changed, chances are that Jesus would have been forgotten, and the Christian church would never have been born. But the Christian church did come into being. Almost two thousand years after these events, Jesus and his teachings are known throughout the world. . . .

The secret of what happened to change this gloomy outlook on the future is recorded in the Scriptures as Luke's account of the Pentecost event. (Acts ch. 2)

The tiny group of frightened disciples was locked in its house. Suddenly, the place is filled with a strange noise like that of a strong wind. At the same time, what seemed to be tongues of fire rested on each of the Apostles. These things were seen as signs of a most mysterious event which was taking place. The Apostles experienced the promised out-pouring of the power of the Holy Spirit.

Filled with this new gift of the Father, the Apostles forgot all fear and went out to proclaim Jesus to the crowds that had been attracted by the strange goings on. They began speaking, and although their listeners were of many different languages, each one heard the words of the Apostles in their own language. . . .

The Apostles proclaimed Jesus as risen from the dead and many of their listeners came to believe in Jesus.

There can be no doubt that a marvellous change has come over the Apostles. They are transformed. Their doubts and hesitations give way to a quiet certitude. Now they truly understand everything that has taken place among them during the past three years.

They now understand the meaning of the teachings and actions of Jesus. They now understand his death and resurrection. . . .

This is just what Jesus had told them would happen: ". . . the Holy Spirit will teach you everything and remind you of all I have said to you." (John 14:26) Or again: "But when the Spirit of truth comes he will lead you to complete truth." (John 16:13) St. Paul also taught: ". . . no one can say, 'Jesus is Lord' unless he is under the influence of the Holy Spirit." (1 Cor. 12:3)

The Spirit establishes between Jesus and the Apostles an intimate communion of heart and lives, such that, the work of Jesus, far from being stopped, begins to grow in the world. . . .

To those who would try to shut them up Peter and John reply: "We cannot promise to stop proclaiming what we have seen and heard." (Acts 4:20) They remembered what Jesus had said: ". . . you will receive power when the Holy Spirit comes on you, and then you will be my witnesses not only in Jerusalem but throughout Judaea and Samaria, and indeed to the ends of the earth." (Acts 1:8)

B. Seven Aids of the Holy Spirit from the Christian Point of View*

". . . you will receive power when the Holy Spirit comes on you, . . ." (Acts 1:8) Christians say that it is not easy to live every day of their lives as true disciples of Jesus Christ. The Holy Spirit comes to help them and strengthen them for this task. This he does through what they call the seven gifts of the Holy Spirit.

The Spirit helps Christians to know Jesus, to understand his gospel, to hear the word of God and be transformed by it. The Spirit also helps Christians to understand what it means "to follow Jesus" in their daily lives. These are the gifts of Understanding and Counsel.

The Spirit gives Christians strength to face the difficulties of living their lives according to the Gospel. To face the evil by which they might offend God. To face the dangers of all the relationships which unite them with each other and to God, so that these relationships will be founded in love. These are the gifts of Strength, Piety and Fear of the Lord.

The Spirit helps Christians to judge and make choices which will be in accord with the will of God for them, and yet made freely. These are the gifts of Wisdom and Knowledge.

C. Spirit—Holy Spirit†

Pneuma is the Greek word most frequently translated in English as "spirit" and, like the English word, it has an extraordinary number of related meanings. In the Bible, these meanings cluster around two poles, the spirit as a term for distinctively human life and for the dynamic activity of God.

The symbols of the sacrament of baptism are shown in this French stained-glass window. The dove represents the Holy Spirit; water, the source of life and cleansing; the candle, Christ; the garment, innocence and new life.

*Adapted from MacDonald, *Celebrate the Spirit As Gift,* p. 49.

†Adapted from Van A. Harvey, *A Handbook of Theological Terms* (New York: The Macmillan Co., 1964), pp. 228–29.

In the Hebrew Scriptures it is God's Spirit that acts in creation, motivates leaders, imparts wisdom, discernment, and holiness, and that inspires the prophets. In short, the Spirit of God is the power and presence of God in the world and, especially, in the history of Israel. It is the Spirit of God that vitalizes man so that man also may be said to have spirit. Spirit, then, becomes a term for the distinctive powers of man (intelligence, will, and emotion) and is synonymous with "soul" and "heart," which were the terms for the seat of human action and life.

In the New Testament, spirit has roughly the same two meanings, the distinctive qualities of human life and the creative activity of God, although the latter comes to predominate because the New Testament, in general, is written in the conviction that in and through faith in Jesus Christ, which is itself the work of the Spirit, the Holy Spirit has come with unique and extraordinary power. . . . Paul employs spirit in reference to the peculiar redemptive power of God at work in Jesus Christ and in the lives of those who surrender their own claims to righteousness and accept God's graciousness. . . .

In general it may be said that the Holy Spirit (1) is the motivating power in the birth, life, and resurrection of Christ; (2) is believed to be a miraculous power, so that miracles and other extraordinary phenomena are attributed to it; (3) is given to man with faith in Christ and is, therefore, not a natural possession but a gift empowering the faithful to live free from the compulsion to sin; (4) is continuous with the "Spirit of Christ"; (5) is something that manifests itself in a new form of life characterized by joy, peace, patience, goodness, faithfulness, gentleness, and self-control; (6) is the author of special and diverse gifts, such as prophecy, teaching, speaking in tongues; but, above all, (7) is that which is active in the love of the neighbor and, hence, is the basis for the unity of the church.

READING 20

Trinitarian Affirmations

A. Matthew 28:19*

Go therefore and make disciples of all nations, baptizing them in the name of the Father and of the Son and of the Holy Spirit.

B. 2 Corinthians 13:14

The grace of the Lord Jesus Christ and the love of God and the fellowship of the Holy Spirit be with you all.

*From *The Common Bible,* Revised Standard Version.

Notre Dame ("Our Lady") in Paris.

READING 21

The Church

LEE SMITH

The creeds speak of a belief "in one holy catholic and apostolic church." But what is the church? The adjectives—*one, holy, catholic,* and *apostolic*—have been defined in various ways by many students of religion; and the many definitions are still the basis of discussion, debate, unity, diversity, and even dissention and conflict. Because the word *church* has been so widely used by Christians who accept the creeds in one way or another and even by those who do not acknowledge the creeds, the concept of the church must be explored in order to gain insight into what Christianity is about.

Learning about the concept of the church is like learning about any other concept. Early in life we learned to identify a chair, but as we grew in years and experienced chairs in their endless variety of colors, sizes, shapes, and materials, our concept of the chair expanded. Likewise, to understand what the church is, we must explore what it has been through the ages and the various expressions of the churches in our own times. In doing so, the meanings of "one," "holy," "catholic," and "apostolic" will also be expanded.

Many people regard the church as a building, and they are right. But it is more than a building. Others consider it a congregation of people, a parish, a geographical district, or an organization such as a conference, synod, or stake; and, depending on their frame of reference, they are all right. Some have looked upon the church as a power structure. Sociologists have analyzed it in terms of systems of statuses or social positions—clergy and laity, each with a set of expected roles or behaviors to perform. To extend this list would serve only to extend confusion.

For a temporary definition of the church we will begin by calling it a *community of people,* ranging from two to almost any number. Usually the community is characterized by a *belief* or *faith* in *one God* who has revealed himself to humanity throughout the ages in three ways—as *Father, Son,* and *Holy Spirit.*

To learn about what the church is today, one must look to its history and identify what it has been in the past. This is important because like other religions, especially Judaism, Christianity has not only affected history, but has been influenced by history. Like Judaism, Christianity holds that God has been at work with humanity in the world. The impact of Christianity on history is obvious, at least to the extent that our present calendar system numbers its years from the traditional birth of Christ.

It would be a task beyond the scope of this study to trace the entire history of Christianity. We shall lighten the load by "stopping the clock" at several points in time to see what is going on in Christianity. This "post-holing" process is less risky if we keep in mind several general guidelines:

1. *History is always interpretation.* The events or so-called facts about events and people are observed, reported, and then given meaning. The process is never complete or pure.
2. *Culture change is ever present.* The sheer fact that people are born and die assures us that change is a constant factor. The speed, intensity, and degree of change may vary considerably.
3. *Culture continuity is real.* While change is a persisting factor, not everything changes completely. Elements of the past are always carried into the present and future.
4. *Culture change and culture continuity are complex.* Seldom do events occur in isolation, and once change or continuity exists, all other aspects of culture are potentially affected. In other words, an event usually has many causes and effects rather than just one.

With these guidelines in mind we will approach the history of Christianity by stopping the clock at certain points on the following time line and examining what was happening at each point in time. The five categories on the time line are treated in subsequent readings.

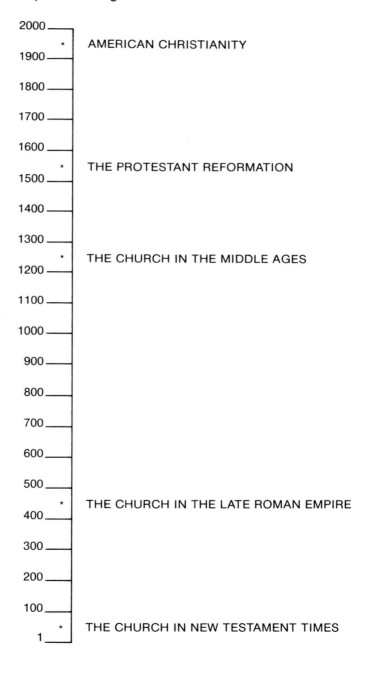

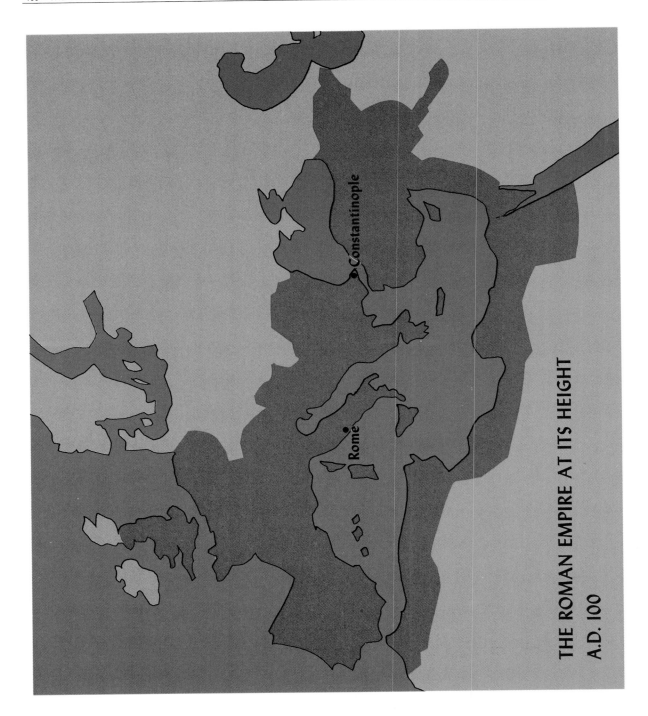

THE ROMAN EMPIRE AT ITS HEIGHT
A.D. 100

READING 22

The Church in New Testament Times

To learn about Christianity in the formative years of the first century, it is important to examine what people were saying and writing about it. The following quotations from the New Testament offer insight into the concept of the church in early New Testament times, or the first century A.D. As you read these quotations, keep in mind the following cautions and questions.

CAUTIONS

1. These passages of Scripture were selected because they are thought to have bearing on the nature of the church. Selection is always dangerous because of the biases of the selector.
2. To limit the reading to a reasonable length, pieces were taken from the whole. Thus there is the risk of "ripping" things out of context.
3. There are always the problems of translation from original languages and of assigning the appropriate meaning to words.

To offset the first two cautions, you may wish to read the larger sections from which the passages were taken. You may also wish to read the same passages in translations other than the Revised Standard Version or *Common Bible,* which is the translation used in this reading.

QUESTIONS FOR THOUGHT AND DISCUSSION

1. What is the church?
2. What is the basis of the church?
3. What are the purposes of the church?
4. What are the essential elements of a church?
5. What is the relation of the church and God? Of Jesus and the church?
6. What kinds of problems, issues, and concerns were showing up in the early church?
7. What was practiced by members?
8. What was expected of members?
9. What kinds of concerns were there about unity and diversity?
10. What analogies or comparisons are used to describe the church?
11. What questions do you have about these selections?
12. Considering the possible interpretations of these passages, what effect might different interpretations have on the answers to some of the above questions?

SELECTED EXCERPTS FROM THE NEW TESTAMENT

In the Gospel According to Matthew we read:

Now when Jesus came into the district of Caesarea Philippi, he asked his disciples, "Who do men say that the Son of man is?" And they said, "Some say John the Baptist, others say Elijah, and others Jeremiah or one of the prophets." He said to them, "But who do you say that I am?" Simon Peter replied, "You are the Christ, the Son of the living God." And Jesus answered him, "Blessed are you, Simon Bar-Jona! For flesh and blood has not revealed this to you, but my Father who is in heaven. And I tell you, you are Peter, and on this rock I will build my church, and the powers of death shall not prevail against it. I will give you the keys of the kingdom of heaven, and whatever you bind on earth shall be bound in heaven, and whatever you loose on earth shall be loosed in heaven." (Matthew 16:13–19)

"Truly I say to you, whatever you bind on earth shall be bound in heaven, and whatever you loose on earth shall be loosed in heaven. Again I say to you, if two of you agree on earth about anything they ask, it will be done for them by my Father in heaven. For where two or three are gathered in my name, there am I in the midst of them."

Then Peter came up and said to him, "Lord, how often shall my brother sin against me, and I forgive him? As many as seven times?" Jesus said to him, "I do not say to you seven times, but seventy times seven." (Matthew 18:18–22)

In the Gospel According to John we read these words of Jesus:

"I am the true vine, and my Father is the vinedresser. Every branch of mine that bears no fruit, he takes away, and every branch that does bear fruit he prunes, that it may bear more fruit. You are already made clean by the word which I have spoken to you. Abide in me, and I in you. As the branch cannot bear fruit by itself, unless it abides in the vine, neither can you, unless you abide in me. I am the vine, you are the branches. He who abides in me, and I in him, he it is that bears much fruit, for apart from me you can do nothing. If a man does not abide in me, he is cast forth as a branch and withers; and the branches are gathered, thrown into the fire and burned. If you abide in me, and my words abide in you, ask whatever you will, and it shall be done for you. By this my Father is glorified, that you bear much fruit, and so prove to be my disciples. As the Father has loved me, so have I loved you; abide in my love. If you keep my commandments, you will abide in my love, just as I have kept my Father's commandments and abide in his love. These things I have spoken to you, that my joy may be in you, and that your joy may be full.

"This is my commandment, that you love one another as I have loved you. Greater love has no man than this, that a man lay down his life for his friends. You are my friends if you do what I command you. No longer do I call you servants, for the servant does not know what his master is doing; but I have called you friends, for all that I have heard from my Father I have made known to you. You did not choose me, but I chose you and appointed you that you should go and bear fruit and that your fruit should abide; so that whatever you ask the Father in my name, he may give it to you. This I command you, to love one another.

"If the world hates you, know that it has hated me before it hated you. If you were of the world, the world would love its own; but because you are not of the world, but I chose you out of the world, therefore the world hates you. Remember the word that I said to you, 'A servant is not greater than his master.' If they persecuted me, they will persecute you; if they kept my word, they will keep yours also. But all this they will do to you on my account, because they do not know him who sent me. If I had not come and spoken to them, they would not have sin; but now they have no excuse for their sin. He who hates me hates my Father also. If I had not done among them the works which no one else did, they would not have sin; but now they have seen and hated both me and my Father. It is to fulfil the word that is written in their law, 'They hated me without a cause.' But when the Counselor comes, whom I shall send to you from the Father, even the Spirit of truth, who proceeds from the Father, he will bear witness to me; and you also are witnesses, because you have been with me from the beginning." (John 15:1–27)

Christ bestowing a blessing.

In the Acts of the Apostles we find this passage in which Peter addresses the apostles.

When the day of Pentecost had come, they were all together in one place. And suddenly a sound came from heaven like the rush of a mighty wind, and it filled all the house where they were sitting. And there appeared to them tongues as of fire, distributed and resting on each one of them. And they were all filled with the Holy Spirit and began to speak in other tongues, as the Spirit gave them utterance. . . .

But Peter, standing with the eleven, lifted up his voice and addressed them, "Men of Judea and all who dwell in Jerusalem, let this be known to you, and give ear to my words. For these men are not drunk, as you suppose, since it is only the third hour of the day; but this is what was spoken by the prophet Joel: 'And in the last days it shall be, God declares, that I will pour out my Spirit upon all flesh, and your sons and your daughters shall prophesy, and your young men shall see visions, and your old men shall dream dreams; yea, and on my menservants and my maidservants in those days I will pour out my Spirit; and they shall prophesy. And I will show wonders in the heaven above and signs on the earth beneath, blood, and fire, and vapor of smoke. . . .'

"Brethren, I may say to you confidently of the patriarch David that he both died and was buried, and his tomb is with us to this day. Being therefore a prophet, and knowing that God had sworn with an oath to him that he would set one of his descendants upon his throne, he foresaw and spoke of the resurrection of the Christ, that he was not abandoned to Hades, nor did his flesh see corruption. This Jesus God raised up, and of that we all are witnesses. Being therefore exalted at the right hand of God, and having received from the Father the promise of the Holy Spirit, he has poured out this which you see and hear. . . ."

. . . And Peter said to them, "Repent, and be baptized every one of you in the name of Jesus Christ for the forgiveness of your sins; and you shall receive the gift of the Holy Spirit. For the promise is to you and to your children and to all that are far off, every one whom the Lord our God calls to him." And he testified with many other words and exhorted them, saying, "Save yourselves from this crooked generation." So those who received his word were baptized, and there were added that day about three thousand souls. And they devoted themselves to the apostles' teaching and fellowship, to the breaking of bread and the prayers.

And fear came upon every soul; and many wonders and signs were done through the apostles. And all who believed were together and had all things in common; and they sold their possessions and goods and distributed them to all, as any had need. And day by day, attending the temple together and breaking bread in their homes, they partook of food with glad and generous hearts, praising God and having favor with all the people. And the Lord added to their number day by day those who were being saved. (Acts 2:1-4, 14-19, 29-33, 38-47)

Also in the Acts of the Apostles we read:

And when they had appointed elders for them in every church, with prayer and fasting, they committed them to the Lord in whom they believed. (Acts 14:23)

And these words of Saint Paul:

"And now, behold, I am going to Jerusalem, bound in the Spirit, not knowing what shall befall me there; except that the Holy Spirit testifies to me in every city that imprisonment and afflictions await me. But I do not account my life of any value nor as precious to myself, if only I may accomplish my course and the ministry which I received from the Lord Jesus, to testify to the gospel of the grace of God. And now, behold, I know that all you among whom I have gone preaching the kingdom will see my face no more. Therefore I testify to you this day that I am innocent of the blood of all of you, for I did not shrink from declaring to you the whole counsel of God." (Acts 20:22-27)

Saint Paul was a first-century convert to Christianity and very active in spreading the religion to many cities in the Mediterranean world. He is credited with a wealth of information in the form of epistles, or letters, which he wrote to these young churches.

To the church in Rome he wrote:

I appeal to you therefore, brethren, by the mercies of God, to present your bodies as a living sacrifice, holy and acceptable to God, which is your spiritual worship. Do not be conformed to this world but be transformed by the renewal of your mind, that you may prove what is the will of God, what is good and acceptable and perfect.

For by the grace given to me I bid every one among you not to think of himself more highly than he ought to think, but to think with sober judgment, each according to the measure of faith which God has assigned him. For as in one body we have many members, and all the members do not have the same function, so we, though many, are one body in Christ, and individually members one of another. Having gifts that differ according to the grace given to us, let us use them: if prophecy, in proportion to our faith; if service, in our serving; he who teaches, in his teaching; he who exhorts, in his exhortation; he who contributes, in liberality; he who gives aid, with zeal; he who does acts of mercy, with cheerfulness. (Romans 12:1–8)

And to the Christians at Corinth he wrote:

Paul, called by the will of God to be an apostle of Christ Jesus, and our brother Sosthenes,

To the church of God which is at Corinth, to those sanctified in Christ Jesus, called to be saints together with all those who in every place call on the name of our Lord Jesus Christ, both their Lord and ours:

Grace to you and peace from God our Father and the Lord Jesus Christ.

I give thanks to God always for you because of the grace of God which was given you in Christ Jesus. . . . God is faithful, by whom you were called into the fellowship of his Son, Jesus Christ our Lord.

I appeal to you, brethren, by the name of our Lord Jesus Christ, that all of you agree and that there be no dissensions among you, but that you be united in the same mind and the same judgment. For it has been reported to me by Chloe's people that there is quarreling among you, my brethren. What I mean is that each one of you says, "I belong to Paul," or "I belong to Apollos," or "I belong to Cephas," or "I belong to Christ." Is Christ divided? Was Paul crucified for you? Or were you baptized in the name of Paul? (1 Corinthians 1:1–4, 9–13)

Therefore I want you to understand that no one speaking by the Spirit of God ever says "Jesus be cursed!" and no one can say "Jesus is Lord" except by the Holy Spirit.

Now there are varieties of gifts, but the same Spirit; and there are varieties of service, but the same Lord; and there are varieties of working, but it is the same God who inspires them all in every one. To each is given the manifestation of the Spirit for the common good. . . .

For just as the body is one and has many members, and all the members of the body, though many, are one body, so it is with Christ . . . .

Now you are the body of Christ and individually members of it. And God has appointed in the church first apostles, second prophets, third teachers, then workers of miracles, then healers, helpers, administrators, speakers in various kinds of tongues. (1 Corinthians 12:3–7, 12, 27–28)

So we do not lose heart. Though our outer nature is wasting away, our inner nature is being renewed every day. For this slight momentary affliction is preparing for us an eternal weight of glory beyond all comparison, because we look not to the things that are seen but to the things that are unseen; for the things that are seen are transient, but the things that are unseen are eternal. (2 Corinthians 4:16–18)

To the church in Ephesus Paul wrote:

I therefore, a prisoner for the Lord, beg you to lead a life worthy of the calling to which you have been called, with all lowliness and meekness, with patience, forbearing one another in love, eager to maintain the unity of the Spirit in the bond of peace. There is one body and one Spirit, just as you were called to the one hope that belongs to your call, one Lord, one faith, one baptism, one God and Father of us all, who is above all and through all and in all. But grace was given to each of us according to the measure of Christ's gift. Therefore it is said, "When he ascended on high he led a host of captives, and he gave gifts to men." . . . And his gifts were that some should be apostles, some prophets, some evangelists, some pastors and teachers, to equip the saints for the work of ministry, for building up the body of Christ, until we all attain to the unity of the faith and of the knowledge of the Son of God, to mature manhood, to the measure of the stature of the fulness of Christ; so that we may no longer be children, tossed to and fro and carried about with every wind of doctrine, by the cunning of men, by their craftiness in deceitful wiles. Rather, speaking the truth in love, we are to grow up in every way into him who is the head, into Christ, from whom the whole body, joined and knit together by every joint with which it is supplied, when each part is working properly, makes bodily growth and upbuilds itself in love. (Ephesians 4:1–8, 11–16)

Writing to Colossians he said:

Now I rejoice in my sufferings for your sake, and in my flesh I complete what is lacking in Christ's afflictions for the sake of his body, that is, the church, of which I became a minister according to the divine office which was given to me for you, to make the word of God fully known, the mystery hidden for ages and generations but now made manifest to his saints. To them God chose to make known how great among the Gentiles are the riches of the glory of this mystery, which is Christ in you, the hope of glory. Him we proclaim, warning every man and teaching every man in all wisdom, that we may present every man mature in Christ. For this I toil, striving with all the energy which he mightily inspires within me. (Colossians 1:24–29)

The following excerpts are from the epistle of James, another early Christian writer.

Count it all joy, my brethren, when you meet various trials, for you know that the testing of your faith produces steadfastness. And let steadfastness have its full effect, that you may be perfect and complete, lacking in nothing. . . .

Blessed is the man who endures trial, for when he has stood the test he will receive the crown of life which God has promised to those who love him. . . .

But be doers of the word, and not hearers only, deceiving yourselves. For if any one is a hearer of the word and not a doer, he is like a man who observes his natural face in a mirror; for he observes himself and goes away and at once forgets what he was like. But he who looks into the perfect law, the law of liberty, and perseveres, being no hearer that forgets but a doer that acts, he shall be blessed in his doing. (James 1:2–4, 12, 22–25)

What does it profit, my brethren, if a man says he has faith but has not works? Can his faith save him? If a brother or sister is ill-clad and in lack of daily food, and one of you says to them, "Go in peace, be warmed and filled," without giving them the things needed for the body, what does it profit? So faith by itself, if it has no works, is dead. (James 2:14–17)

The crown of eternal life.

A Roman statue of Constantine the Great.

READING 23

The Church in the Late Roman Empire
LEE SMITH

The rise of the church parallels the decline and fall of the Roman Empire. For nearly two hundred years following the birth of Christ the Roman Empire remained large and enjoyed reasonably good health. Following the death of Emperor Marcus Aurelius, A.D. 180, the empire began to demonstrate complex problems from which it never did recover.

The government grew increasingly wasteful, inefficient, and ineffective. The loyalty of the army was no longer assured. Generals, one after another, succeeded in overthrowing the government and setting themselves up as emperor, only to be replaced by others in the same manner. Representative government, once the pride of the Romans, existed no longer. Rome was losing land and building walls to save what it could. Communication, administrative, legal, and judicial systems based on efficiency and justice gave way to graft, corruption, and increasing distrust. Historians can cite only a few emperors who attempted to improve the situation. Political assassination added to the instability; twenty of twenty-two emperors were assassinated between the years 235 and 284.

If political problems seemed bad, those of the economy were worse. Massive unemployment added an increasing number of people to the welfare roles each day. As upper-class people lost influence in the government, they fled to the rural areas and attempted to establish themselves as landlords. This resulted in a higher concentration of land in the hands of a few. Small farmers fled to the cities to collect welfare "doles" of "bread and cir-cuses."[1] Others became the captive slave laborers of the landed aristocracy. Farming became more inefficient. Food shortages increased and so did food prices. Inflation became so bad and the money so worthless that the government refused to take its own money for taxes. Taxes threatened to ruin everyone. Trade de-clined as highway robbery and piracy on the high seas increased because military protection and courts of justice declined.

Two emperors stand out for having tried to deal with the problems of Rome. Diocletian, who ruled from 284 to 305, attempted to revamp the administrative system. He created a large secret service to detect graft and corruption in the huge government bureaucracy. Great pomp and mysticism came to surround the emperor in the time of Diocletian as an attempt to dazzle and awe the subjects. The emperors came to be treated as gods in the flesh.

Constantine emerged from the power struggle that followed the retirement of Diocletian in 305. It took Constantine nearly twenty years to consolidate the power which he held until his death in 337. Constantine is marked by his conversion to Christianity, his issuance of the law that assured toleration for Christians, and his convening the Council of Nicaea. He turned his attention to economic conditions by establishing ceiling prices and by making all jobs hereditary and movement from one farm to another or one trade to another illegal.

In the time of Constantine it was becoming more apparent that the eastern half of the empire had far more vitality and strength. Constantine built a new capital city in the east, at the ancient Greek town of Byzantium. He named the city "New Rome" but it soon became known as Constantinople. Today this city is known as Istanbul. It is important to note that Constantine was taking the initiative to save a crumbling empire. He moved the capital to the east in hopes of pumping the lifeblood of the east into the entire empire. The greatest impact of the move, however, was to divide the empire in two—east and west. From 395 on, they were never united again. The eastern half became known as the Byzantine Empire and it survived another thousand years beyond the col-lapse of the Roman Empire in the west.

---

[1]"Circuses" refers to various entertainments including games and sports.

In the west conditions continued to worsen. The efforts of Diocletian and Constantine had no effect on saving the empire. As political, social, and economic problems remained unresolved, the moral decline deepened. The moral decay was more than bad manners, sin, or whatever. In its simplest form it was a disintegration of relationships—between men and women, parents and children, soldiers and superiors, government and citizens. The peace, security, prosperity, legal and social justice once known in the Mediterranean world no longer existed. It was

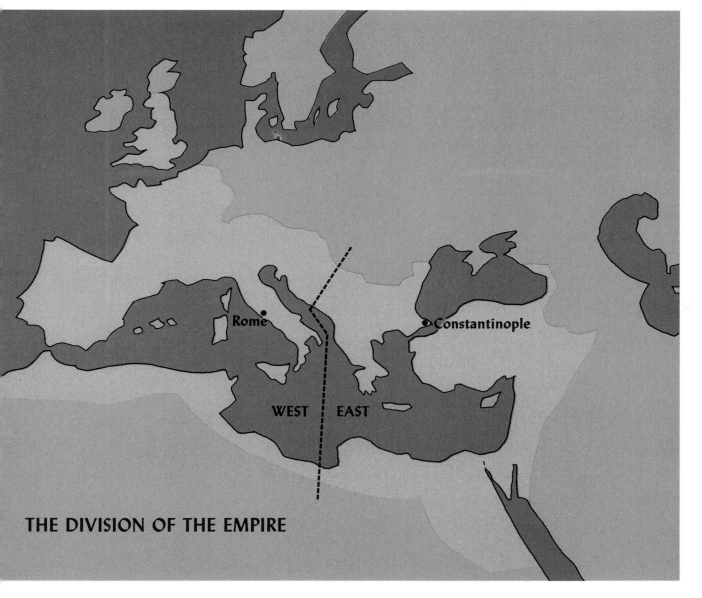

Rome

Constantinople

WEST ¦ EAST

THE DIVISION OF THE EMPIRE

an age of chaos, weakness, and vulnerability. In short, it was an age of insecurity. Again, people fled wherever they could for security. Some fled to the country for land, some to the cities for welfare. Some sought to escape or find themselves in philosophical or religious systems. There was a continuing search for a new start, new meaning, new life, for hope, peace, and security. While this persistent search went on, there were a large number of new religions and philosophical systems emerging in the Roman world. Not the least of these was Christianity.

The Romans saw Christianity as a Jewish sect in Palestine. To be sure, questions were raised during the first century: Was Jesus the promised Messiah of the Jews? Was he the son of God? Was he king of the Jews? Was he raised from the dead? The answers to these questions varied with whoever was answering them. There had been a wide range of interpretation of the Messiah in Judaism.

When the Roman Empire was strong, it tended to leave the religions of a local area alone. Jews and Christians, however, were suspect from the outset because of their belief that there was only *one God.* This precluded either of these two groups from worshipping the emperor as a part of the Roman Pantheon. As the Christian movement grew it tended to pose more of a threat to the Roman emperors who were trying to strengthen their hold on the people. The situation resulted in bloody persecutions of the Christians until at least 313 when Constantine issued the Edict of Milan by which Christianity was officially tolerated.

In spite of persecution the movement continued to grow as Christian communities or congregations were established throughout the Mediterranean world. We have seen the efforts of St. Paul to keep these communities informed through letters and to help them settle disputes. As the year 200 approached there emerged priests or presbyters as the heads of local congregations, and a bishop as the overseer of all the congregations and their priests in a given city. Theoretically, all bishops were equal because their authority had been derived from the apostles or representatives of the apostles. But the bishops of the wealthier, more prestigious cities such as Jerusalem, Antioch, Alexandria, Constantinople, and Rome gained prominence and influence.

That there were differences in the communities and their beliefs, even during the first century, is generally accepted. These differences were often related to local cultures and languages of the people. Pre-Christian practices were Christianized and continued. The celebration dates of Christmas provide an example. The differences continued to grow until it became apparent that conflict would break out in the church. Constantine, for whatever his motives might have been, decided to deal with the problem. In 325 he summoned the first ecumenical council, or council of bishops, which met in the city of Nicaea. By initiating the council Constantine had done an even greater thing than he had when he issued the Edict of Milan in 313. For now, the state had begun to meddle in the internal affairs of the church. Which was Constantine more concerned with, Christian unity or his own political power, or a degree of each? Perhaps more important is the fact that the Council of Nicaea issued the Nicene Creed in an attempt to unify the Christian doctrine of the Trinity. Thus the power of church and state stood face to face. Councils were now to be seen as an authoritative decision-making body in matters of doctrine and church teaching.

But what was the appeal? Why did so many people become Christians in the first four centuries? Certainly the fact that the Roman Empire (at least in the west) was in trouble produced a crisis which caused people to look for outside solutions to problems. Another explanation might be found in the actions of Constantine. It can be argued that the zeal and enthusiasm of the apostles and St. Paul resulted in mass conversions. Perhaps the best way to come to grips with this issue is to consider who the converts to this new religion were. In general, the greatest number of converts came from the lower classes—slaves, women, and soldiers.

The appeal to the lower classes can be seen in the very message of Christianity—its teaching that all men are equal in the sight of God, the notion of a loving Father who sent his Son to die for the sins of man in order that man might have eternal life, and its promise of hope in what seemed to be a hopeless life and world. Love for fellow men under the fatherhood of God and the release of fear and guilt helped the Christian gain a feeling of a new birth into life.

As Christianity spread along the great road system of the Roman Empire, it was not only the lower classes of society who latched onto it, but also some of the great, curious, and intelligent minds of the time. One can cite individuals such as Ambrose,

Jerome, and Augustine. St. Augustine, who lived from 354 to 430, was the son of a pagan father and Christian mother. He grew up moving from one philosophical system to another. His life of great searching led him into all the vices of the Roman world, as well as its ideas. He later came to take Christianity quite seriously. Following his conversion he became a very productive writer and effected a most profound impact on Christian theology. In his work *The Confessions,* Augustine disclosed his personal spiritual quest and its attainment. In the *City of God,* he defended the church against its antagonists who were accusing the Christians of causing the fall of Rome. Augustine argued that history revealed God's plan and that the real event would be the triumph of the "City of God" over the "Earthly City" of those who had rejected God. His writing, whether correctly or incorrectly interpreted, was to have a marked impact on Western civilization.

As time went on the bishops of major cities such as Rome, Constantinople, Antioch, Jerusalem, and Alexandria gained power and influence. As religious leaders of these major cities they became the overbishops, archbishops, or patriarchs of the churches, bishops, and priests in the surrounding area. In the absence of effective court systems and judicial systems, people turned increasingly to the church's leadership for resolving disputes. Matters of doctrine and belief were brought to the church and usually to the bishop. In time, the bishop of Rome came to be seen as a court of last resort, especially in matters of faith and doctrine. But not all the bishops of the church were willing to place so much authority in the hands of the Roman bishop. The bishops of the east, particularly Constantinople, refused to give such obedience to Rome; but in the western half of the empire, the bishop of Rome had complete authority over all other western bishops. One of the major reasons for this is the Petrine theory, which is based on the interpretation of Matthew 16:18–19 according to which Peter was given power by Christ as the first bishop of Rome. Peter passed his power as bishop of Rome to his successors. Herein we have the origin of the pope. The churches in the east, known as the Eastern Orthodox churches, refused to accept this authority, and with this and other differences the churches of the east and west grew further apart until they clearly split in 1054.

READING 24

The Church in the Middle Ages

A. The Rise of the Medieval Church

LEE SMITH

Historians still debate when the Middle Ages or medieval period in western European history existed. Its beginning is variously dated from approximately 200 to 500, its conclusion from 1200 to 1500; and some have said much of the medieval period is still with us. In any case, the period refers to a time between the classical period of Greece and Rome and the modern period marked by the commercial revolution, the development of the national state in Europe and its expansion into colonial empires, the Renaissance or "new birth" in art, literature, philosophy, and science, and the Reformation of the western church. The medieval period refers exclusively to western Europe and is characterized by its looking in upon itself. Examples of this introspective and myopic view can be seen in the self-sufficient agricultural community called the manor and the castle or fortress with its walls, moat, and dungeon. Whether the medieval period was a time of decline or a time of new beginnings can be argued with increasing vigor as the period continues to be studied. One of the abiding dreams of the period was the hope of restoring the unity and power of the old Roman Empire. This dream of returning to "the good old days" became the goal of kings, princes, bishops, and popes. The goal of empire building (imperialism) is not totally absent today.

We have seen that with the decay and collapse of the Roman Empire there was created a political vacuum in Europe. No longer was there a system of justice in courts of law or protection on the roads to encourage trade. These were wiped out with the fall of the Roman administrative system. People sought other institutions for security—the manor, feudalism (protection based on local ties), and the church.

The church, from its beginnings in Palestine, had enjoyed a steady growth throughout the Roman Empire during periods of severe persecution and later under toleration until it reached the point where emperors adopted the church and attempted to use it to save their sagging empire. From the outset the church had diversity in belief and practice. The differences increased, especially between the churches of the east, where Greek was used as the language of the church and where there was a reluctance to accept the supremacy of the bishop of Rome. While the empire in the east was to remain intact with periods of health and strength until 1453, the empire of the west had officially collapsed by 476.

In their attempts to use the church in the west to strengthen the falling empire, the emperors had tried to make the church as unified as possible. Because of these events, the church in the western half of the empire emerged in the Middle Ages with the following characteristics:

1. A concern for unity of the "whole church"
2. An intimate relationship with the state
3. A power structure or centralized administrative system very much like that of the old Roman Empire (see following chart)
4. An accepting recognition of the bishop of Rome (the pope) as the superior authority

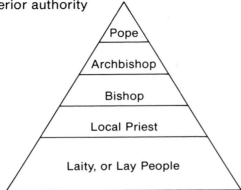

Pope
Archbishop
Bishop
Local Priest
Laity, or Lay People

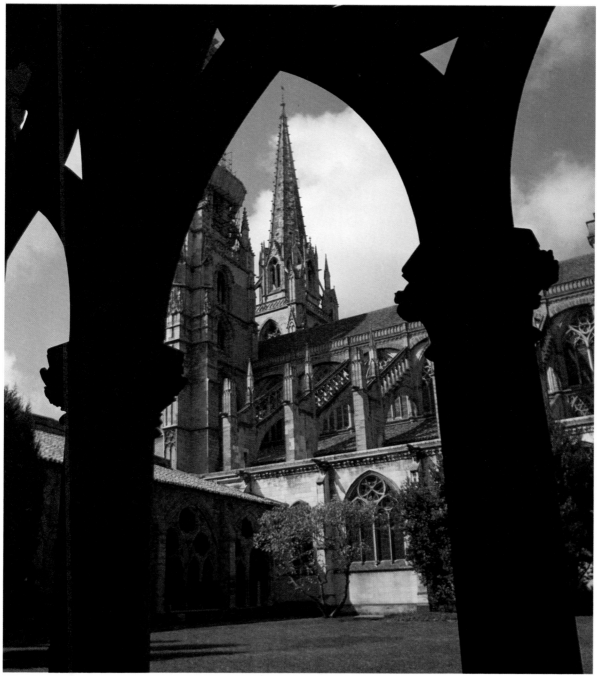

This is a medieval cloister next to a large cathedral. Priests used to take walks along such cloisters, saying their daily prayers.

With a few short-lived exceptions, such as during the reign of Charlemagne, medieval Europe remained a hodgepodge of walled-in little kingdoms, each trying to strengthen itself by getting the favor of the pope, manipulating the bishops in the area, or making war on its neighbor. Meanwhile, the rest of the world was not idle. The Byzantine Empire (eastern half of the Roman Empire) enjoyed periods of stability, strength, and prosperity. The Eastern Orthodox churches had grown increasingly independent of the churches in the west. They had a well-developed tradition and vitality both before and after their formal separation from the west in 1054. In Arabia, a man named Muhammad was born around 570; and between the years 622 and 732 the new religion which Muhammad formulated—Islam—was to spread through Persia, Egypt, North Africa, Spain, Portugal, and the southern half of France. Charles Martel, a Frankish ruler and the grandfather of Charlemagne, was able to check the advances of Islam in Europe at the Battle of Poitiers (Tours) in 733. From this time on it was to take over seven hundred years to drive the Muslims from western Europe.

Some historians have contended that the real inheritor of the old Roman Empire was the church in the west. In the absence of civil authority and civil courts people turned to the church as the most neutral, universal, and respected agency. The church was conducting legal activities and formulating law. The relationship of church and state, started in the fourth century by Constantine, continued to grow. When there were strong leaders in the empire, the church was subject. When the emperor was weak and the bishop of Rome strong, the empire was subject. There were, of course, times when both were weak and other times when both were strong.

Princes, dukes, and large landholders with some military strength sought to make themselves king in their area; but usually, in the fashion of Charlemagne, they sought the blessing of the pope to rule. When it came to investiture (the process of naming the bishops of an area), both kings and popes fought for control over this privilege. The case of Henry IV (ruler of what is now a part of Germany) illustrates the issue. Henry had been excommunicated by Pope Gregory VII because of his continued persistence in appointing bishops. The following letter, in which the pope describes his encounter with Henry, illustrates the magnitude of the pope's power.

Henry IV Goes to Canossa[1]
(Letter: *Gregory to the Bishops,* 1077)

Gregory, Bishop, servant of the servants of God, to all arch-bishops, bishops, dukes, counts, and other princes of the kingdom of the Germans, who defend the Christian faith—greeting and apostolic blessing.

Since, from your love of justice, you have made common cause with us and shared our peril in the struggle of Christian warfare, we have taken pains, with our sincere affection, to inform you, beloved, of how the king, humbled to penitence, obtained the pardon of absolution. . . .

As was arranged with the envoys, whom you sent to us, we came into Lombardy about twenty days before the date on which one of the nobles was to meet us at the pass. We awaited the arrival of the escort so that we might be able to cross to your land. But when the date had passed and we learned that it had not been possible for you to send an escort to meet us, we were indeed perplexed as to what we had better do, since we had no means of crossing over to you.

In the meantime we learned for certain that the king was coming. Before he entered Italy he sent suppliant messengers to us and promised to render satisfaction in all things to God, to St. Peter, and to us. Moreover, he promised to amend his life and to maintain complete obedience, if only he might be considered worthy to obtain the grace of absolution and apostolic blessing from us.

We had many consultations with him by messenger, during which we upbraided him severely for his evil deeds. At last he came in person. He had but few attendants and no air of hostility or defiance when he came to Canossa, where we were waiting.

There he laid aside all royal state. For three days he remained at the gate of the castle, wretched, barefooted, and clad in wool. He continued with much weeping to implore the aid and consolation of the apostolic mercy until he moved all who were there or who heard of it to such pity and compassion that they all interceded for him with many prayers and tears. They were astonished by the unusual hardness of our minds. Some even said that we were showing not the weighty severity of an apostle but the cruel ferocity of a tyrant.

At last, overcome by his persistence and by the urgent prayers of all present, in the end we loosed the bond of the anathema [formal

[1]From Paul L. Hughes and Robert F. Fries, *Readings in Western Civilization* (Ames, Iowa: Littlefield, Adams & Co., 1956), pp. 26–27.

ban issued by the church] and admitted him to the grace of communion. We received him again into the bosom of the Holy Mother Church.

We can further see the grip of the pope's power in the following statement.

Dictatus Papae Gregorii VII[2]

[The so-called *Dictatus Papae Gregorii VII* was drawn up ca. 1075. Its authenticity has been questioned, but the weight of opinion attributes it to Gregory VII and regards it as probably a private memorandum. At all events, this list of the principal prerogatives claimed by the papacy is, as Voosen says (*Papaute et pouvoir civil a l'epoque de Gregoire VII*, p. 71), 'a syllabus of the ideas which thenceforth were to dominate all the history of the pontificate.' . . .]

The Council of Macon, convened in A.D. 585 by order of King Guntram, King of Orleans, Burgundy. Among other things, the Council determined the relative importance of clerics and laymen.

That the Roman church was founded by the Lord alone.

That only the Roman pontiff is rightly called universal.

That he alone can depose or reestablish bishops.

That his legate [official representative], even if of inferior rank, is above all bishops in council; and he can give sentence of deposition against them.

That the pope can depose the absent.

That, among other things, we ought not to remain in the same house with one whom he has excommunicated.

That it is permitted to him alone to establish new laws for the necessity of the time, to assemble new congregations, to make an abbey of a canonry [a chapter of priests serving a cathedral]; and on the other hand, to divide a rich bishopric and combine poor ones.

That he alone can use imperial insignia.

That all princes kiss the feet of the pope alone.

That his name alone is recited in the churches.

That his name is unique in the world.

That it is permitted to him to depose emperors.

That it is permitted to him to transfer bishops, under pressure of necessity, from one see [jurisdiction] to another.

That throughout the church, wherever he wishes, he can ordain a cleric.

That one ordained by him can be over the church of another, but not to perform service; and that he ought not to accept a superior rank from any bishop.

[2]Adapted from Ewart Lewis, *Medieval Political Ideas,* Vol. 2 (New York: Cooper Square Publishers, 1974), pp. 380–81. Originally published by Alfred A. Knopf, 1954.

That no synod not summoned by him ought to be called general. . . .

That his decision ought to be reviewed by no one, and that he alone can review the decisions of everyone.

That he ought to be judged by no one.

That no one may dare to condemn a man who is appealing to the apostolic see.

That the greater cases of every church ought to be referred to him.

That the Roman church has never erred nor will ever err, as the Scripture bears witness.

That the Roman pontiff, if he has been canonically ordained, is indubitably made holy by the merits of the blessed Peter. . . .

That by his precept and licence subjects are permitted to accuse their lords.

That he can depose and reestablish bishops without a meeting of the synod.

That he who is not in concord with the Roman church is not held to be a catholic.

That he can absolve the subjects of the unjust from their fealty [loyalty].

The political power of the church is especially apparent in the leadership of the pope with regard to the Crusades.

Pope Urban's Speech at Clermont Concerning the Crusades Against the Moslems[3]
(Robert the Monk, *Urban's Speech,* 1095)

Oh, Franks, race set apart and blessed by God, set apart from all other races by the situation of your country, as well as by your faith, we wish you to know what a grievous cause has led us to your country, and what peril threatens you and all the faithful.

From Jerusalem and the city of Constantinople a terrible tale has come to us, namely, that a race from the kingdom of the Persians, an accursed race, a race alienated from God, has invaded the lands of those Christians and has depopulated the Holy Land by the sword, rapine [plunder], and fire; it has led away a part of the captives into slavery and a part it has destroyed by inhuman tortures; it has destroyed the churches of God or taken them for the rites of its own religion. They destroy the altars, after having defiled them. They circumcise the Christians and the blood of the circumcision they either spread on the altars or pour into the baptismal font.

[3]From Hughes and Fries, *Readings in Western Civilization,* pp. 30–31.

When they wish to torture people by a base death, they perforate their navels, and dragging forth their intestines, bind them to a stake; then with whipping they force the victim to walk until the viscera runs forth and the Christian dies. Others they compel to extend their necks, bared, and compete to see which can cut through the neck with a single blow. On whom therefore is the labor of avenging these wrongs if not on you? You, upon whom above other nations God has conferred remarkable glory in arms, courage, and strength to humble those who resist you.

But if you are hindered by love of children, parents and wife, remember what the Lord says in the Gospel, "He that loveth father or mother more than me, is not worthy of me."

Jerusalem is the navel of the world; the land is fruitful above all others, like another paradise of delights. While your land is shut in on all sides by the seas and surrounded by the mountains and is too narrow for your large population; nor does it abound in wealth. Therefore, enter upon the road to the Holy Sepulchre; wrest that land from the wicked race, and subject it to yourselves.

When Pope Urban had said these and other things he so influenced to one purpose the desires of all who were present that they cried out, "It is the will of God! It is the will of God!"

And Urban, lifting his eyes to heaven said, "Unless the Lord God had been present in your spirits, all of you would not have uttered the same cry, therefore, let that be your motto and battle word, "It is the will of God."

Moreover, therefore, whoever shall determine upon this holy work shall make his vow to God as a living sacrifice, and shall wear the sign of the cross of the Lord on his forehead or on his breast. When having fulfilled his vow he returns to his own domain let him place the cross on his back between his shoulders.

The leadership of the church, at all levels, involved itself with the economy quite as much as it did with political affairs. The late Professor Hoyt of the University of Minnesota points this out in the following excerpt.[4]

The Church taught that people engaged in trade should avoid the sin of avarice [greed]. They should charge a "just price" for their goods, this being defined as the cost of the material plus the value of the labor expended on it. Any higher price was uncharitable to one's neighbor (the buyer), and the good Christian was expected to give to charity the difference between the just price and any higher price at which he sold. . . .

[4]From Robert S. Hoyt, *Europe in the Middle Ages,* 2d ed. (New York: Harcourt, Brace & World, 1966), pp. 447–48, 355.

The teaching of the Church on usury was also based on the concept of avarice as a sin. Anyone who could lend money was assumed to have more than he needed for his own livelihood; anyone who borrowed was assumed to be too poor to sustain himself—else why should he want to borrow? Under these circumstances, to lend freely was a charitable act, but to charge interest on the loan was to take advantage of another's poverty. Today usury means exorbitant interest; in the early Middle Ages any interest at all was called usury, and even the lowest interest rate was considered morally exorbitant. But the facts were rapidly outstripping the moral teaching of the Church. Most of the men who sought loans were not charity-fed paupers but businessmen and manorial lords who needed capital for commercial or agricultural enterprise, or nobles who were living beyond their normal means to keep up the proper appearances. The most important borrowers of all were governments. When political policy or military exigencies required castle building along frontiers or the fortification of towns, such projects could not be paid for out of ordinary revenues. The only recourse was to borrow money against future income, and this could be done only by paying interest. Even the papal government, while deploring usury, found it necessary to borrow heavily and pay interest. . . .

. . . The pope collected taxes and dues as temporal ruler of the Papal States, received income from the estates and other property with which the see of St. Peter was endowed, and collected revenues of various sorts as head of the Church. Among the latter were fines and fees charged in the normal course of judicial administration, revenues paid by exempt monasteries and bishops, taxes levied on the clergy in support of crusades and for other purposes, and a variety of payments from clergy and laity alike ranging from the gifts of pilgrims in Rome to extraordinary fees for special services or privileges. Although papal income grew rapidly under Innocent III and his successors, the *curia* [administration governing the church] and its expenses grew even more.

Monks receiving feudal lords at the door of a monastery.

As the power of the church and its leaders grew in politics and economics, the church became instrumental in broadening the gap between the social classes. Position in society was based on ties of land, military and personal loyalty, and craft or trade. The church taught that all humans were equal before God; however, the idea did not seem to apply in everyday life as much as it did in life after death. The following two selections demonstrate the social distinctions in medieval Europe.

The Orders of Society[5]

This selection from the eleventh century describes the organiza-
tion of society as it was understood by Adalberon, the Bishop of
Laon and an adviser to Hugh Capet, king of France from 987 to 996.

The clergy forms one order in society. It is governed by church
law. Two other orders are governed by civil laws. They are the noble
and the nonnoble.

The nobles are the warriors and the protectors of the churches.
They defend all people, rich and poor. As a matter of fact, they even
protect themselves.

The nonnoble class does not enjoy the freedom of the noble
class. This unfortunate group obtains nothing without suffering. It
provides food, clothing, and other supplies for everyone in the
society. No free man can live without unfree men.

The class distinction between nobles and serfs is well understood. But, what is harder to understand is the extreme social
distance among the clergy.

A Medieval Diocese

Adalberon stated that the clergy made up one order of society.
The following account provides evidence about the lives of clergy-
men in the twelfth century.

The bishop and his aides conducted the affairs of the Church
from the administrative center of the diocese.[6] The administrative
center was always the city where the bishop's cathedral was built.
Among the bishop's aides were a chancellor of the diocese who
supervised the cathedral school, the treasurer who looked after the
financial affairs of the diocese, and the archdeacon who presided
over the Church court. Priests and deacons assisted these officials.

The donations of the nobles, the offerings of the peasants either
in money or produce, and the income from the bishop's benefice[7]
permitted the bishop and his most important officials to live very
comfortably. They were able to buy fine robes, ornaments, and
other luxuries. The bishop also supported a number of charitable
causes in his diocese. Many bishops devoted more than half of their
income to maintaining cathedral schools, building parish
churches, and supporting the poor.

---

[5]This and the following selection are from Adalberon, *Carmen ad Rothertum Regem,* as
quoted in Robert Boutruche, *Seigneurie et Feodalite* (Paris: Aubier, 1959), pp. 371–72.
Translated by John M. Good in *The Shaping of Western Society: An Inquiry Approach* (New
York: Holt, Rinehart and Winston, 1968), pp. 70–71.

[6]A diocese was the basic administrative unit of the Church. It was divided into parishes.

[7]Benefice, here, refers to the property or fixed income attached to high Church offices.

During the Middle Ages, great cathedrals and churches loomed over every town, testifying to the importance the townspeople gave to religion and the Church.

In addition to administering Church affairs, the bishop also assisted the nobles of his diocese. He advised them on government policies, settled differences between competing nobles, and served as an ambassador to the courts of other noblemen.

The boundaries of a parish were usually the same as the boundaries of a manor. The parish was supervised by a priest selected by the lord of the manor with the approval of the bishop. He was generally drawn from the ranks of the local peasantry. Most parish priests attended the cathedral school only long enough to learn to read the Scriptures and the liturgy of the mass. They could not afford the extensive education that noblemen received to become bishops. The priests performed the services in the manor church and spent much of their time ministering to the needs of the peasants. They often acted as family doctors and lawyers as well.

The wealth and power that accumulated at all levels of the church was used in many ways. To be sure, some of it was squandered on personal and vain projects of the church leaders, but much of it was put into constructive and helpful endeavors. One of the most enduring contributions came in the form of architecture. The great Romanesque and Gothic cathedrals built during medieval times stand as memorials to the laborers, craftsmen, artisans, architects, priests, and bishops whose muscles and minds brought about their existence. Cathedrals and the works of art they contained presented illiterate people with messages about their God, their heritage, their present life, and their life to come. The purpose of the cathedrals, music, and the arts was to glorify God and point man to heaven. In this way the church was providing opportunity for artists and craftsmen to use their talents.

Any social entity or group, if it grows and passes its culture to the next generation, will in all probability develop some form of organization to serve its members, to accomplish its goals, and to educate the next generation. Thus it was natural for the early church to organize its resources and energies to accomplish its tasks. It was reasonable that it would organize its bureaucracy or administration along the lines of the Roman system, for it was the most apparent model to copy. It is quite believable that the leaders of the church, being human, would range from excellent to disgraceful. Any organization which accumulates power and wealth runs the risk of using them unwisely.

From early times there is evidence that certain individuals and groups differed on various aspects of Christianity. The areas of disagreement ranged widely from matters of doctrine or teaching (Nicene Creed) to decision making and use of authority (the bishop of Rome and ecumenical councils). There were, through the ages, Christians who thought the leaders of the church were corrupt and more concerned with the affairs of this world than with spiritual matters. Within the framework of the church some wanted simplicity in church matters; others wanted to lead a life of contemplation away from the noise and temptation of the world. These concerns and desires gave rise to the establishment of various monastic orders.

One of the early leaders of monasticism in Christianity was St. Basil (329–379). He set forth three rules for monastic life: hard labor, works of charity, and communal life. His ideas spread from Asia Minor to the west. Around 520, St. Benedict (480–543) founded a monastery named Monte Cassino and established the rules of poverty, obedience, and chastity. These rules, combined with communal life, hard work, meditation, study, and prayer, were to constitute the monks' *opus Dei* (the work of God). As time went on, monasteries became lax in their discipline; many acquired wealth. New reforms and new orders of monks were established to correct the situation. Two very prominent orders of monks developed in the thirteenth century in protest of the worldliness of the church. One order, known as the Franciscans, was founded by St. Francis of Assisi (1181–1226). The other, the Dominicans, was founded by St. Dominic (1170–1221). Both of these orders emphasized poverty, begging, work, contemplation, prayer, and service to God and fellow humans. In doing the "work of God" monks served society not only with prayer and acts of charity but also with the preservation of knowledge. The community of monks spent great energy copying manuscripts, producing art, and developing new knowledge such as improved agricultural techniques.

B. What It Meant to Be a Christian in the Middle Ages*

T. WALTER WALLBANK AND ALASTAIR M. TAYLOR

We have described the church as a power structure, its growth in numbers and area, its authority, accumulation of wealth,

*From T. Walter Wallbank and Alastair M. Taylor, *Civilization: Past and Present*, Vol. I, 3d ed. (Chicago: Scott, Foresman and Co., 1954), pp. 391–94.

and aesthetic activities. Most Europeans were automatically born into the church by virtue of the fact that there was no alternative. What was it like for the typical person? How did the church function to meet the needs of the people it served? The following two selections shed light on these questions.

THE CHURCH'S METHODS OF SALVATION

The purpose of the Church. The Church was the agency of Christ. It alone could interpret and carry out the instructions of its founder. It alone possessed the means necessary for salvation. The individual was helpless and could not secure salvation without belonging to the Church. In a word, the Church was the essential intermediary between God and man.

The Middle Ages had as a primary objective the preparation for an afterlife. To die safely rather than to build up earthly treasures or gain fame was the goal of every true Christian.

According to the Church, salvation was gained through the performance of certain ceremonies. These were found mainly in the sacramental system. The nature and process of salvation was expounded by an elaborate system of thought known as theology—the evaluation of man's relationship to God, together with the study of the reasons for man's existence. It should be noted that a unified system of theology scarcely took definite shape until the thirteenth century, when canon law, papal administration, and the works of such theologians as Peter Lombard, Albert the Great, and St. Thomas Aquinas established a fairly harmonious system of theology.

Theology. Salvation was the object of living, and therefore the main tenets of medieval theology center about the means of achieving salvation. Man had originally lived in a state of perfection. But Adam and Eve of their own free will fell from the perfect state and so lost Paradise. Furthermore, Adam bequeathed to his children the taint of original sin, and they bequeathed it in turn to their descendants. Thus all the human race was damned from the outset. Jesus, the Son of God, sacrificed Himself upon the cross at Calvary in order that He might atone for the sins of mankind, and through His sacrifice God again gave to man an opportunity to win eternal perfection. But—and this was paramount in the mind of every medieval person—salvation was won only by the

Contributing to the Church as a means of honoring God was a duty and an honor for everyone in the Middle Ages. These details from stained-glass windows in the Cathedral of Chartres show some of the various tradesmen who donated money for the windows (glaziers, teamsters, wheelwrights, and furriers).

grace of God, and salvation came only to the man who believed in redemption through the atonement made on the cross by Christ.

Each man, therefore, had to act if he were not to be damned forever. However, since he could perform no act worthy of salvation without divine grace, how was this to be earned? The theologians taught that God bestowed His grace on man by means of the Church and its officials, for (according to the Petrine theory) the successors of Peter held the very keys of salvation. The Church created definite ceremonies by which men secured grace. These ceremonies are known as sacraments, "the outward and visible signs of invisible grace."

The sacraments. By the twelfth century, these sacraments had been limited to seven, a number made official in the fifteenth century.

As Pope Eugene IV wrote in 1438: "There are seven sacraments under the new law: that is to say, baptism, confirmation, the mass, penance, extreme unction, ordination, and matrimony . . . these our sacraments both contain grace and confer it upon all who receive them worthily."[1]

In *baptism* the taint of original sin was washed away, and the person was given a Christian name (hence "christening"). *Confirmation* took place during the period of adolescence and was intended to strengthen the character of the youth during his formative years. *Penance* was designed to remove personal sins committed after baptism. Penance depended upon three elements. The first was contrition, which involved a turning away from sin and a sense of shame. The second was oral confession, in early times made publicly, but later made to a father confessor. The third element was satisfaction, by which the penitent made restitution for his wrongs in any way which his confessor suggested, such as prayer, fasting, almsgiving, or pilgrimages. For those penalties imposed but not discharged before death, a stay in purgatory was necessary.

The most important sacrament was the *Holy Eucharist,* or Lord's Supper. In the Fourth Lateran Council of 1215, the full teaching of the Church regarding the Eucharist was set forth. The dogma of "the real presence of the incarnate Christ by the process of transubstantiation" was there affirmed. No proper appreciation of the ceremony of the Mass can possibly be obtained unless the significance of transubstantiation is understood.

[1]J. H. Robinson, *Readings in European History* (Boston: Ginn and Company, 1906), p. 159.

According to this doctrine, when the priest pronounces over the bread and wine the age-old words of Christ, "For this is My body. . . . For this is the chalice of My blood," a miracle takes place. To all outward appearances, the bread and wine appear unchanged, but in "substance" they have been transformed into the very body and blood of the Saviour. The laity used to receive both the wine and the bread. However, the spilling of the wine—now become Christ's blood—led to the practice of the priest drinking the wine for them.

Marriage was sanctified by a sacrament. The Church preferred celibacy as an ideal, but without marriage there would soon be no Church at all. Marriage within certain degrees of family relationship was strictly forbidden.

Extreme unction was the sacrament administered at the time of death and was designed to give the Christian comfort as to his chances of salvation, by removing from him the remains of sin, except, of course, those unatoned for, requiring an interval in purgatory.

The seventh sacrament was that of *holy orders,* or the ordination into the priesthood. It was administered by the bishop and gave the priest virtues which made him distinct from secular men. The ordained priest was capable of making possible the miracle of transubstantiation as well as performing the other sacraments. Therefore the clergy (through the sacrament of ordination) became an integral part of the system which insured mankind's salvation.

The religion of the common people. The problems of theology attracted the attention primarily of the intellectuals. The majority of the people then, as today, accepted the beliefs of the world in which they lived without very much questioning. To the unlettered population, the following constituted the essentials of the Christian faith: (1) the Creation and Fall of Adam, (2) the birth and the crucifixion of Christ, (3) the Last Judgment, (4) the horrors of hell, and (5) the eternal bliss of heaven. The sacramental system promised a safe entrance into heaven. Then why worry needlessly over fine points of theology?

HOW THE CHURCH ENFORCED ITS TEACHINGS

The weapons of the Church. The weapons the Church used to implement its teachings and commands were very effective indeed. The principal ones were (1) canon law, (2) excommunication, (3) interdict, and (4) command of vast revenues.

Canon law. Canon law had been developed from the Scriptures, the writings of the Church Fathers, the disciplinary and doctrinal rules made by church councils, and the decrees of the Popes. The collection of these canons resulted in many problems and contradictions. The *Digest* of Justinian's Code was found in the eleventh century, and thus Roman law was studied afresh. In the following century (1140) a monk named Gratian compiled his famous code *Concordia descordantium canonum* (harmony of conflicting canons), known generally as the *Decretum.* Ultimately, the Church issued its official body of canon law, known as the *corpus iuris canonici.* This represents the ecclesiastical counterpart to the Justinian Code, known as the *corpus iuris civilis.*

Canon law protected the clergy from laymen. Every man who had been admitted to the clerical state and could read and write enjoyed what is known as benefit of clergy. This meant that a churchman could be tried only in church courts according to canon law, in spite of the fact that he might have committed a serious crime against a layman. This practice led to serious abuses, for the clergy usually got off with lighter punishments in their own courts.

The Church used canon law to punish such crimes as perjury, blasphemy, sorcery, usury, which the medieval Church denounced, and heresy,[2] the most horrible of all crimes in medieval eyes. A murder was a crime against a fellow man, but disbelief in the teachings of Christ or His Church was a crime against God Himself.

The Inquisition. In the thirteenth century, the Church devised an institution known as the Inquisition to cope with a rising tide of heresy and to bring religious conformity to Europe. These heresies were certain schools of thought which questioned the basic doctrines of the Church or argued that salvation could be attained by methods different from those officially prescribed by the Church. The Inquisition was an elaborate system of inquiry into the beliefs of persons suspected of being heretics. People accused of heresy were tried in the court of the Inquisition. If an accused person confessed and abjured, or renounced, his heresy, he was "reconciled" with the Church on performance of penance.

[2]A point of view opposed to the official position or teaching. Thus a heretic is one who questions or opposes the official teachings and practices.

The Last Judgment was portrayed above the doors of thousands of medieval churches, indicating the attention given to attaining salvation.

If he did not voluntarily confess, he could be subjected to torture, one of the most commonly used forms being the rack, which wrenched the limbs of the victim. If torture failed to make the prisoner confess, he was declared a heretic and turned over to the secular authorities (unless he abjured in the meantime) to be burned at the stake.

Few scholars have been able to look at the Inquisition objectively. Some have condemned it completely, while others have tended to minimize its errors. It must be kept in mind that Roman law had made use of torture and that Roman emperors often ordered condemned persons to be burned at the stake. Furthermore, to the medieval mind the soul was infinitely more important than the body. Therefore the torturing of a suspected heretic was justifiable if by confession his soul could be saved from certain hellfire. The great French scholar of the Inquisition, Jean Guiraud, has analyzed some 930 inquisitional sentences pronounced between 1308 and 1323. He found that 42 persons, or between four and five per cent of the cases, were sentenced to death; 139 persons (about fifteen per cent) were acquitted. The remainder were either imprisoned or assigned various penances.

Excommunication. But the Church generally made use not of outright physical punishments but of spiritual penalties. The most powerful of these was excommunication, which simply meant exclusion from the Church. If a man would not heed the commands of the Church, he was excommunicated. It was a very serious penalty, for *extra ecclesiam nulla salus*—outside the Church there is no salvation. Excommunication might vary in its punishment. At its worst it banned the victim from all participation in the ritual of the Church, denied its spiritual help, forbade other Christians to associate with him or help him in any way, freed all his vassals from their oaths of fealty [loyalty] to him, and prevented his burial in consecrated soil. The attending ceremony added solemnity and terror to the punishment. On occasion the bishop appeared, attended by twelve priests, each holding a lighted candle. At the moment when the curse, or anathema, was declared, the candles were dashed to the ground to signify the extinction of the guilty one's soul.

Here are the concluding lines of a thirteenth-century Scottish excommunication directed against enemies of the Church.

"Accursed be all the forenamed persons; cursed be they without and within, from the sole of the foot even to the crown of the head. And may their part and companionship be with Dathan and Abiram whom the earth swallowed quick.[3] May their days be few and their offices let others take; may their children be orphans; and as this light is at this moment extinguished, so may the lights of their lives be extinguished before the face of Him who liveth for ever and ever; and may their souls be plunged in hell unless they repent and amend their ways and make satisfaction. So be it! So be it! Amen! (The candles are extinguished, and a bell is rung.)"[4]

Interdict. Excommunication was directed against single persons; interdict punished whole groups in localities. The interdict has been termed "an ecclesiastical lockout." In the country or territory thus penalized, no church services were held, and all sacraments save baptism, penance, and confirmation were withheld. The interdict was a most powerful weapon, one instrumental . . . in bringing King John of England to his knees and forcing him to give his entire kingdom to the Pope, getting it back as a fief [on condition of homage to the Pope].

Church revenues. The main revenues which the Church received were (1) donations, (2) tithes, (3) fees, and (4) feudal dues. For centuries kings and nobles were generous contributors to bishoprics and monasteries. The lands given to the Church were said to have fallen *in mortua manu,* or into the clutch of a dead hand *(mortmain),* because the Church kept perpetually all lands which were donated to her. Kings saw their wealth disappearing alarmingly from such bequests. Finally in England in the reign of Edward I the famous Statute of Mortmain was passed in an attempt to put an end to this loss of wealth.

The tithe, which means one tenth of a man's income, was the regular income of the priest. In the twelfth century Pope Alexander III extended the tithe until it was levied on forests, mills, and even the labor of artisans. The common people came to resent the levying of tithes very much, especially when the taxes went to clergymen who remained absent from their residences among the people.

---

[3]Dathan and Abiram led a group of Israelites in a rebellion against Moses and Aaron. As God's punishment, they were swallowed up alive into the earth (see Numbers 16:1-33).
[4]David Patrick, ed., *Statutes of the Scottish Church,* 1225–1559 (Edinburgh: Edinburgh University Press, 1907), p. 4.

Fees for the performance of religious services and for the administration of some of the sacraments were another source of wealth. Revenue also came from the payment of feudal dues by vassals to bishops and abbots who were feudal lords and from the payment of manorial dues by peasants to churchmen who possessed manors. ... The growing wealth of the Church, the greatest landowner in medieval Europe, brought about many abuses and a worldliness among the clergy which weakened the faith of the common people.

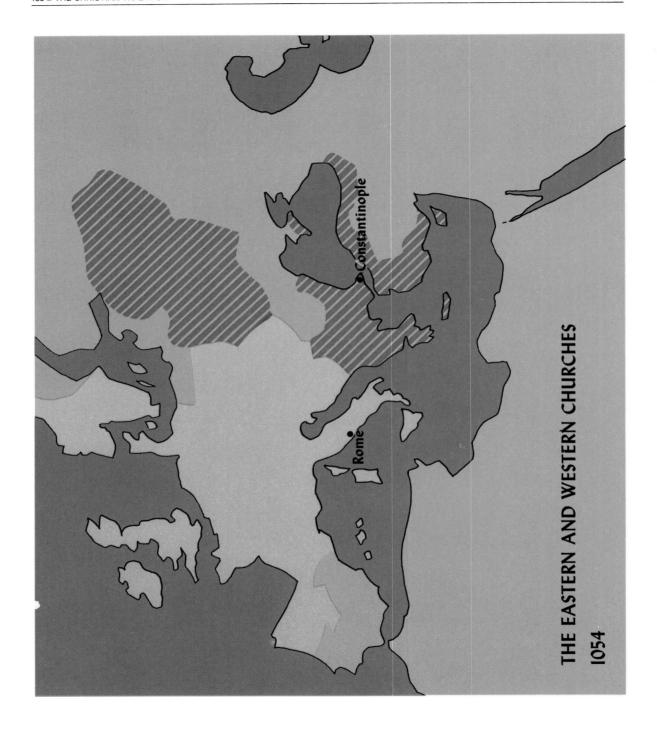

THE EASTERN AND WESTERN CHURCHES

1054

Constantinople

Rome

READING 25

A Climate for Reformation
LEE SMITH

In its first one thousand years the church had grown from a small group of "fired-up" individuals in Palestine to a major religious movement, spreading its influence throughout the Middle East, eastern and western Europe, and points beyond. As it grew in membership, it also grew as an administrative organization. From the outset there had always been variation and diversity among individual churches, and that was not to change. As the power structure in the western church expanded and the differences between the churches of the east and west increased, a division was bound to occur. In 1054 the separation of the churches in the east and west became official and irreparable. The pope and the patriarch of Constantinople excommunicated each other, a ban which was not to be lifted until 1965. The church of the west came to be known as Roman Catholic or Latin; the churches of the east, as Greek Orthodox and later, as other national identities emerged, as Russian Orthodox, Syrian Orthodox, and so on.

And so the "body of Christ," the church universal, had been officially ripped in two. But there was more to come, this time in the fracturing of the western church. The period of European history in which this took place is called the Reformation, a term which refers to the "explosion" in the western church during the sixteenth century. The churches of the east have not experienced a similar reformation to this date.

The Reformation has been called the Protestant Reformation and the sixteenth-century Reformation. Both terms are accurate to a certain degree, but both are misleading as well. The term *Protestant* has been used to categorize all groups of Christians who are not Roman Catholic or Eastern Orthodox. Some so-called Protestants, however, have more in common with the Roman Catholic church than with other Protestants. For example, Lutherans and Baptists are both Protestant, but Lutherans are probably more like Roman Catholics than they are like Baptists. The most important reason why the term *Protestant* is probably inappropriate for the Reformation is because most people categorized as such are not now protesting the Roman Catholic church.

Limiting the reformation of the western church to the sixteenth century is also improper, because doing so fails to take into account the fact that the reforming process had been going on within the church for centuries, through new monastic orders, canon law, writings, and council and papal decisions. The sixteenth-century Reformation, however, was a powerful revolt that left in its path a sizable number of Christians who were no longer regarded as members of the Roman Catholic church.

It is important to remember that events like the Reformation do not occur in a vacuum. They are not usually the work of a single individual, nor can they usually be separated from a series of related events. With this in mind, let us examine some of the events and trends that foreshadowed the Reformation period of history.

Beginning with Pope Urban's plea for the first Crusade to liberate the Holy Land from the Muslims and his hope to regain control of the eastern churches (Orthodox), Europeans began to come increasingly out of their isolation. The Crusades exposed them to a world of new ideas, land, products, money, and languages. Europe was breaking out of its shell. By the 1200s, some of the monastery and cathedral schools had developed into universities as great centers of learning. These centers were concerned not only with preserving and passing on existing knowledge, but with furthering and discovering new knowledge. Scholarship was thus expanding and gaining new respectability.

While the Crusades accomplished little for the church and failed in the military sense, they did succeed in stimulating mobility and trade, making money increasingly available. As the

The power of the popes was both spiritual and temporal, as the massive fortress castle of the popes at Avignon clearly demonstrates.

merchants became a new source for kings to tax, kings gained power and wealth. This permitted them to buy and provide the services and protection of central government more as it is known today. The kings began to get expansionist ideas for new lands, new products, and new wealth. The Columbus expedition of 1492 is representative of the times. The center of the world had shifted from the Mediterranean Sea to the Atlantic Ocean. The focus of people's attention had shifted from life after death to the affairs of this life—not that people would no longer look to an afterlife, but that the emphasis would shift increasingly toward a view that this life should be lived in a fulfilling way too.

In this age of restlessness the decisions and policies, as well as the very basic teachings of the church, were to come under repeated questioning and criticism in many circles, especially in university settings. One of the abuses that the church had been criticized for was its worldliness—its concern with the affairs of this world rather than with the spiritual needs of its people. Among other abuses the church was charged with were selling religious offices (often to the highest bidder), selling the sacraments, and meddling in the affairs of secular government. The clergy were accused (and rightly so, at times) of being immoral. As previously noted, various monastic orders originated in an attempt to cleanse the church of its worldliness and excesses (see p. 129). This monasticism was a reforming force within the church over a period of several centuries.

Moreover, there had been a series of events that caused people to question the authority of the church. This issue was prompted by rising kings who squabbled with the pope over the appointment of bishops, taxation, and a host of other issues. From 1309 to 1376 the popes were under the influence of the French monarchy to the extent that they actually lived in Avignon, France. This situation was resented by the English, Germans, Scandinavians, Irish, and others. From 1378 to 1409 there were two popes, one ruling from Rome and the other from Avignon. Then for another eight years there were three popes. Finally, in 1417, the Council of Constance succeeded in deposing all three popes and electing a fourth, restoring the sole papacy to Rome. Thus church leaders, through representative councils, had some measure of success in reforming the church and resolving problems. The power of such councils to initiate reform, however, was later prohibited by the pope.

The people who questioned the church and its practices were either accommodated within the church, were persuaded to yield to the church, were excommunicated, or were driven out as heretics. Some who actually tried to reform the church often met harsh treatment—even death. Among such reformers were John Wycliffe (England, 1324?–1384) and John Huss (Bohemia, 1369?–1415). These men advanced the ideas that services and the Bible should be in the language of the people, that salvation was between the individual and God rather than the church, that some of the church rituals were idolatrous. Although Wycliffe was severely denounced by the pope for his heretical ideas, Huss, because of the strong influence he exerted, was burned at the stake. However, the ideas of men like Wycliffe and Huss were kept burning for a century and set into a blazing explosion by a German priest in 1517.

*Martin Luther. After a painting
by Lucas Cranach, the elder.*

READING 26

The Reformation
LEE SMITH

The Reformation comprised a complex series of events which shattered the structural unity of the Christian churches in the west. It set into motion a process which has continued to manifest itself to the present time. Generally the causes of the Reformation, other than specifically religious ones, can be grouped into four categories as follows:

Economic Causes. There was considerable resentment against the large amount of land and other wealth held by the church. Businessmen resented the restrictions of the church against profit making and lending of money for interest. Kings and princes who were anxious to consolidate their power objected to the large amounts of money leaving their area in the form of gifts to the church and especially to Rome. Many people resented the vast sums of money the church was spending on buildings, arts, and luxury, particularly among the leadership.

Political Causes. Rising kings and princes resented the church's interference in their affairs of state. Both kings and popes wanted the power to appoint bishops. Both had their eyes on the same wealth as a source of income.

Social Causes. People became increasingly aware of the social distance that existed between human beings—between serf and lord, laity and clergy, priest and bishop. If all were truly equal in the sight of God, if Christ had really died to save all humanity, why then should such vast differences exist among people?

Intellectual Causes. The Crusades, the universities, the monasteries, the discovery of new lands and peoples—all contributed to an increased sense of curiosity about this world and this life. Increased intellectual stimulation fed the fires of curiosity about religion, theology, the afterlife, the Bible, and other sacred writings. This new interest in learning was to get an extra "shot in the arm" with the invention of the printing press with movable type.

At the risk of oversimplification, this discussion of the Reformation centers on five movements: Lutheranism, Calvinism, Anglicanism, Anabaptism, and the Catholic Reformation. Each of these movements entails a complex history of personalities and events too extensive for a detailed investigation in the present study. Only the unique characteristics of each movement will be considered.

LUTHERANISM

Lutheranism originated with the activities of a devout Catholic priest named Father Martin Luther (1483–1546). He was a learned Augustinian monk and a professor of sacred theology at the University of Wittenberg, Germany, in 1517.

Luther came to believe that the words of St. Paul in his Epistle to the Romans ("The just shall live by faith") described the essential requirement for salvation—faith in the validity of Christ's sacrifice, which alone could wash away sins. Unaware of the full implications of this idea, Luther was challenged by the church. Eventually he was forced to take a stand from which he would not or could not retreat. This resulted in his excommunication from the church. There can be no doubt about his disappointment over this, because he dearly loved the church and seems to have wanted only certain reforming actions *within* the church.

Having been excommunicated, he surely would have suffered a fate similar to Huss's and that of other heretics had he not been supported by German princes who were sick of papal interference and money flowing to Rome. Outside the Roman church, Luther had little choice other than to organize his followers into the church which came in time to bear his name.

Among the reformers Luther was mild, and, in many ways, advocated limited change. He remained very near the Roman position on many matters. The following are characteristics which tend to distinguish the spirit of Lutheranism:

1. The Liturgy, Eucharist, or Holy Communion service followed that of the Roman tradition but was translated into the language of the people.
2. The Bible was translated into the language of the people, and its study was encouraged.
3. Two sacraments were to have prominence—Holy Baptism and Holy Communion. The other Roman sacraments—confirmation, confession, ordination, marriage, and ministry to sick and dying—were retained but given the status of "rites."
4. Regarding the Roman doctrine of transubstantiation in which the bread and wine were changed into the body and blood of Christ, Luther taught that the believer does in fact receive the body and blood of Christ through bread and wine.
5. A great heritage of worshipper participation through singing of hymns was developed.
6. Lutherans continued to accept the historical creeds of the church. Additional summaries of belief and practice were set forth in Luther's catechism and other confessional statements, the best known of which is the Augsburg Confession. However, the ultimate source of doctrine was the Holy Bible.
7. Lutheranism developed a highly confessional or creedal system of theology.
8. Clergy were permitted to marry.
9. Since Luther and his followers were now outside the Roman church, a new ecclesiastical structure had to be created. In its European form it did not vary a great deal from the Roman model; however, the authority of the pope was removed.
10. Lutheranism caught on in much of Germany, especially in the north. Denmark, Norway, Sweden, Finland, Latvia, Estonia, and Iceland were soon to follow. In most of these countries, Lutheranism became the "official" state or national church.

CALVINISM

Calvinism had its roots in Switzerland, in the work of Ulrich Zwingli (1484–1531). Zwingli was also a priest, educated at the University of Basel. Though he and Luther differed in tempera-

John Calvin. A copy of a painting by Hans Holbein.

ment, they did share some of the same ideas. However, Luther and Zwingli differed so sharply on the doctrine of Holy Communion that the unity of the Reformation was shattered from 1529 on. Zwingli contended that the sacrament of Holy Communion was a devout commemoration of Christ's death and work and that the bread and wine were merely signs, or symbolic. Luther, on the other hand, stood much closer to the Roman position in which the believing communicant did receive the body and blood of Christ. This difference in interpretation resulted in another separation—Lutheran vs. Reformed.

Zwingli's ideas spread throughout Switzerland, and in 1536 the movement gained the new leadership of John Calvin (1509–1564). Calvin was born and educated in France. His studies moved from the priesthood to law and to the humanities. In sympathy with the Reformation, he found more freedom in Switzerland than in France. Calvin picked up on the work of Zwingli and wrote the *Institutes of the Christian Religion* in which he clearly set forth many of the doctrines for much of so-called Protestantism. Some ideas were held in common with the Lutherans, such as the sole authority of the Bible, the sinfulness of humanity, and the inability to save one's self, hence, salvation by faith in Christ. Some Calvinist distinctions are as follows:

1. Calvin tended to remove everything from the Roman church that was not commanded by the Bible. Luther, on the other hand, permitted everything not forbidden by the Bible.

2. Calvin's position on the Lord's Supper acknowledged the spiritual presence of Christ in the sacrament. This position was between that of Zwingli and Luther.

3. Calvinism became unique in its doctrine of predestination, which teaches that, though salvation is by faith, only those predestined by God can be saved. In other words, faith is a gift of God and is not given to all; as a result, not all can be saved. Calvin contended that the "chosen" are known because of their good works and their striving to keep the law and that they have a divine mission to refashion the morality of their world and build a "Christian community." In attempts to build this model community in Geneva, Switzerland, an extremely rigid moral code was developed to regulate church attendance, dress, luxuries, and especially frivolous behavior like dancing and playing cards. The "model community" in Geneva barely survived one generation beyond Calvin himself.

4. Calvinism recognized two sacraments—Holy Baptism and the Lord's Supper. These were to be more symbolic than in Lutheranism and Romanism.
5. The reading, study, and interpretation of the Bible were highly emphasized and encouraged as an individual responsibility.
6. Calvin's reforms tended to be more radical than those of Luther. Ceremonies of the church were simplified rather than liturgical. Vestments, candles, altars, statues, symbols and art were in many cases stripped from the churches and forbidden since the Bible did not command them.
7. Stark simplicity in worship and strict standards of moral conduct were to become the hallmarks of many Calvinists.
8. In general Calvinists accepted and used the ancient creeds of the church and have developed additional confessional statements, such as the Helvetic Confession, Westminster Confession, and the Heidelberg Catechism.
9. While no single Calvinist organization exists, Calvin's influence was most extensive. Leaders of the so-called Protestants came to Geneva from all over Europe to learn his theology. The Huguenots, or French Reformed church, and the Dutch and Christian Reformed churches are based on Calvinist theology. John Knox carried Calvinism to Scotland where, in time, the movement came to be known as Presbyterianism. It was characterized by a new form of church government in which representative councils governed church affairs. Historically the Puritans were rooted in Calvinism, and they carried its influence into North American denominations like the Congregationalists and the United Church of Christ. Calvinist theology has also influenced the Baptist churches and to some extent the Anglican (Episcopal) and Lutheran churches.

ANGLICANISM

The Anglican church or Church of England, known as the Episcopal church in the United States, is also a product of the sixteenth century. It began when King Henry VIII, in a personal squabble with the pope over a divorce question, declared himself head of the English church. Although this break with Rome and the pope received great support in England, Henry made no attempt to initiate other reforms in the church.

It was under the rule of Henry's daughter, Elizabeth I, that the English church was to receive reform in its teachings and practices. The influence of Luther and Calvin was felt in England. Elizabeth was decidedly in sympathy with the Protestant movement, but she loved the ritual of the Catholic church. She chose a middle ground which sought to preserve much of the Catholic tradition. She, in fact, sought to make the national church both Catholic and Protestant, a position upheld by the English people. It is from this point that permanent reforming trends began and have persisted in terms of the following Anglican characteristics.

1. The historical creeds (Apostles' and Nicene) form the basic doctrine and belief of the Anglican church.

2. Anglicans believe in the apostolic succession, whereby the power of Christ, layed on the Apostle Peter, has been handed down successively from generation to generation.

3. The word *episcopal* is derived from the Greek word *episkopos,* meaning "bishop." It refers to a system of church government by bishops.

4. Anglicans have retained a great deal of the Roman ritual in their services. Thus Anglican services tend to be highly liturgical and formal, although there is some variation in local practices.

5. All seven sacraments are observed by Anglicanism; however, Holy Baptism and Holy Eucharist (Communion) have special prominence. Anglicans, like Roman Catholics and Lutherans, believe in the "real presence" of Christ in Holy Communion.

6. Anglicans use the *Book of Common Prayer* as the basis for their worship. The eloquence of its liturgical use of the English language has been widely acclaimed. Many of its prayers and forms have been borrowed by other English-speaking denominations.

7. Although personal acceptance of the creeds has been the sole standard for church membership, the individual is permitted a wide range of philosophical positions within Anglicanism. The Anglican church has frequently regarded itself as the bridge between Roman Catholics and the so-called Protestant Christians. Its diversity is reflected in a range of liturgical practices from "low" church to "high" church, the latter being very close to Roman Catholic and the former having considerable simplicity. The range in theology can also be great; one can be

"high" church in worship and liberal in theology, or vice versa. From the outset some English people felt that too much of the Roman tradition had been continued. These people came under the influence of Calvinism; and while some preferred to purify the Anglican church further (Puritans), others separated completely (Separatists). These Calvinist groups were among the earliest immigrants to the United States, and their ideas were to have a marked impact on U.S. Christianity.

8. In 1729 John and Charles Wesley originated another reform movement in the Church of England which led to the development of the Methodist church. It too was to have a profound impact on the American scene. But by and large, most English people remained in the Anglican church. Anglicanism was carried to other lands by English emigrants. In Canada the Anglican church retained that name, but in the United States it came to be known as the Episcopal church.

ANABAPTISM

A fourth strain of the Reformation in Europe is that of Anabaptism. It is probably the most difficult part of the movement to describe because it lacks the unity of the other movements as can be seen in its characteristics:

1. Anabaptism was the most radical of the four movements in that it lashed out against most of the practices of the Roman church. It felt the Anglicans, Lutherans, and even the Calvinists had not gone far enough with the reforming process.

2. The most universal characteristic of the Anabaptists was rejection of infant baptism and the belief that a valid baptism could not take place until the individual had an inward experience of regeneration—"a dying in Christ and rising with Him in newness of life."

3. Many people in this movement looked to the millenium in which Christ would come and rule among the truly baptized for one thousand years. During this period, they believed, everyone would live as equals in a society that would be neither rich nor poor.

4. Anabaptists looked toward a "prophetic" leadership that would gather them together in triumph over the pagans, including other "Christians."

5. The movement began and spread from three centers—Switzerland, southern Germany, and Moravia. Everywhere its adherents were to encounter opposition from Roman Catholics, Lutherans, and Calvinists alike. Most Anabaptists agreed that the "true church" was bound to be small and to suffer persecution.

6. Anabaptists believed that the church must be pure. To keep it that way, it must be constantly purged by banning the unworthy, it must remain totally independent of the state, and it must be a select, voluntary society.

7. In spite of persecution, the Anabaptists were strong missionaries. When banished, they felt the need to return and to continue to testify. Every Anabaptist man and woman was expected to carry out missionary work and testify.

8. They saw the church as a gathered society. Those who did not exemplify the pattern of Christ were to be expelled from the church.

9. Anabaptists are ardent pacifists, refusing even to carry weapons of any type.

10. As advocates of the separation of church and state, they refused to take oaths or to participate in public politics.

11. Two early Anabaptist leaders were Menno Simons, founder of the Mennonites, and Jacob Hutter, founder of the Hutterites. The Amish also came out of this tradition. These groups established tight communities and succeeded in perpetuating their own culture, independent of much of the world around them.

12. The word *Anabaptist* means "re-baptized" and is essentially a persecution name given them in Reformation time by their opposition. They preferred the term *Baptist* because they did not consider infant baptism valid. Even if one had been baptized as an infant, adult or believer baptism was not really a re-baptism.

Menno Simons. Woodcut by C. van Sichem, 1605.

13. Rather than remaining in Europe, most Anabaptists moved to new frontiers. Many came to the United States where they exerted extensive influence on both religious and political institutions.

THE CATHOLIC REFORMATION

The Roman church of western Europe was dealt a severe blow in the sixteenth century. It had lost its international and universal grip on the Europeans. Although it remained vital in Italy, Austria, Belgium, France, Ireland, Spain, Portugal, and Poland, in other countries strong national churches had emerged. Northern Germany and Scandinavia were Lutheran; England was Anglican. The Calvinists could claim the Presbyterian church in Scotland and the Reformed churches in Switzerland and the Netherlands. Influences were spreading with the increased movement of people, and the reforming spirit was not to be stopped, even in the new national churches.

What was the Roman church doing during this period of time? At first it was defensive in its reaction to the rising new religious groups. But as time passed, leadership changed and there was increasing concern over some of the problems that existed within the church itself.

The Council of Trent (1545–1563) sought to deal with many of these problems. One of its greatest endeavors was to clearly define the doctrines of the Roman church, thus proving that the church would not compromise with the Protestants on any point of doctrine. For example, the council fixed the number of sacraments at seven, rejected Luther's doctrine of justification by faith alone, and specified that only the Latin Vulgate version of the Bible was authoritative. The Bible and traditions, as interpreted solely by the church, were accepted as the basis of Christianity. A list of heretical books, called the Index, was published, and members were forbidden to read them.

The council went to great length to correct the immorality and administrative problems within the church. Strict discipline of priests and church leaders eliminated many of the former abuses. Thus the council erased many of the abuses that had motivated the Reformation.

A new religious order, founded in 1534 by Ignatius Loyola, was also concerned about the church. This order, called the Society of Jesus, or the Jesuits, sought to regain those people who had wandered from the Roman church. The Jesuits possessed great scholarly traditions and were most effective in establishing schools, especially in the western hemisphere. Their emphasis on education served to upgrade the quality of the priesthood and church leadership.

And so it was that the long and steady growth of power in the western church came to an end in the sixteenth century. The all-embracing unity of the church in the west was lost. National churches emerged in some European countries, while other countries remained loyal to Rome. It was also in this period that massive emigration of Europeans to North America was to begin. The emigrants left the various European countries for a variety of reasons—political, economic, social, and intellectual. For many, emigration meant a new freedom to practice religion according to individual choice and conscience. Thus a new experiment in religious freedom and pluralistic society was launched in North America.

Reading 27

Ranking Christian Denominations in the United States and Canada

The maps on pages 156–57 show the distribution of the major Christian denominations in the United States and Canada. The map of Canada is based on data in *Population: Religious Denominations,* which contains figures from the 1971 Census of Canada, published by Statistics Canada (September 1973).

The percentages shown on the map of the United States are based on data reported in *Churches and Church Membership in the United States: 1971,* by Douglas W. Johnson, Paul R. Picard, and Bernard Quinn (Washington, D.C.: Glenmary Research Center, 1974). An explanation of how denominations were grouped into families for computing percentages is given in the introduction of this report.

Note that on both maps, when no church had 25 percent of the membership in a given area, that area is left blank. When two or more churches had 25 to 49 percent of the membership in a given area, the church having the larger (or largest) membership is shown.

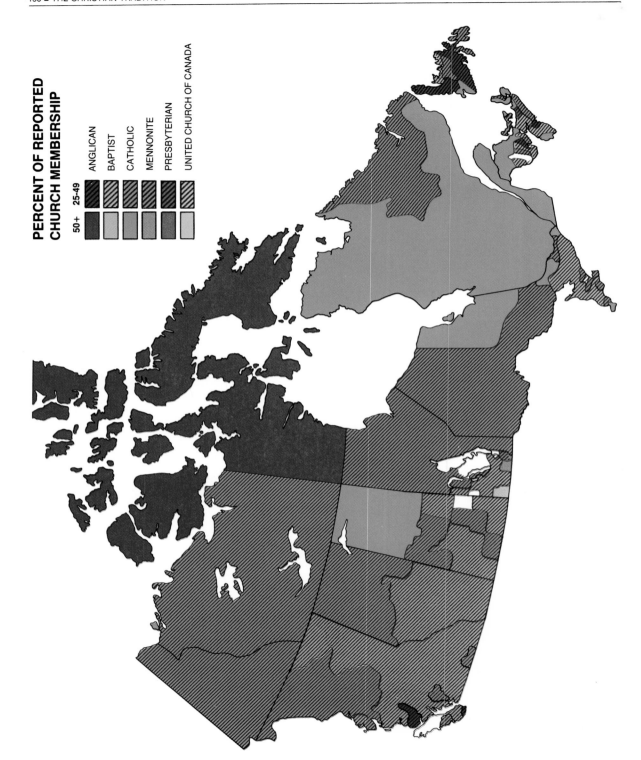

PERCENT OF REPORTED
CHURCH MEMBERSHIP

50+   25-49

ANGLICAN
BAPTIST
CATHOLIC
MENNONITE
PRESBYTERIAN
UNITED CHURCH OF CANADA

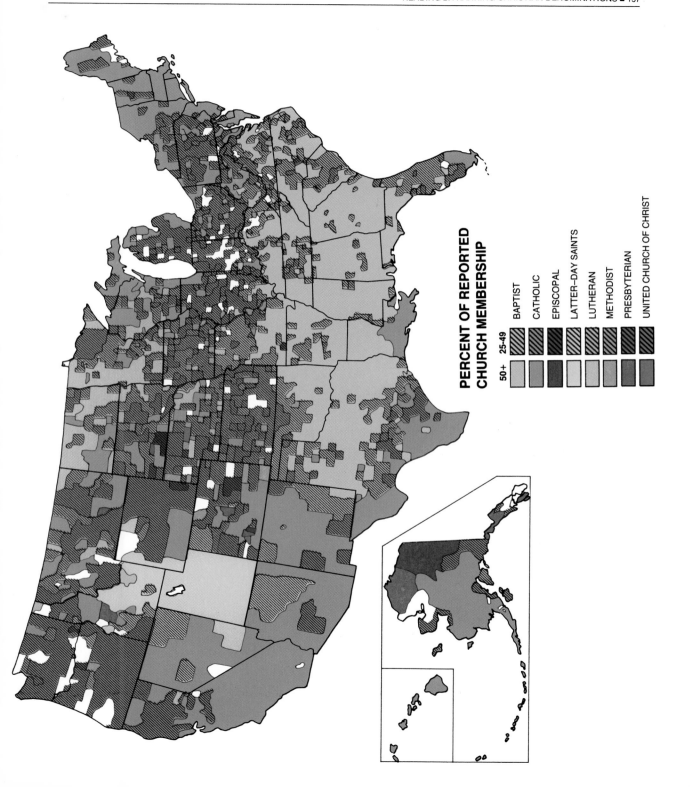

PERCENT OF REPORTED CHURCH MEMBERSHIP

50+   25-49

BAPTIST
CATHOLIC
EPISCOPAL
LATTER–DAY SAINTS
LUTHERAN
METHODIST
PRESBYTERIAN
UNITED CHURCH OF CHRIST

People in sparsely settled western Virginia depended upon traveling preachers to conduct public worship. The people assembled about once a year and formed a religious encampment such as this one.

READING 28

American Christianity
ROBERT W. ROSS

EXPLORATION AND SETTLEMENT

The explorers and early settlers in the Age of Discovery and in the Age of Settlement, or colonizing of the New World, carried forms of Christianity with them. The Spanish explorers of Florida, the Southwest, and California, as well as the French explorers of the Great Lakes region and the Mississippi River, were Roman Catholic. Roman Catholic priests accompanied the expeditions and were among those who settled in these regions.

English and Dutch explorers and settlers were from a variety of Protestant traditions, all of them closely linked to the Protestant Reformation. The English were Anglican, or Church of England (Protestant Episcopal after the Revolutionary War), Puritan, Presbyterian, Congregationalist, Separatist, and, in Maryland, Roman Catholic. The Dutch in New Amsterdam (New York) brought the Dutch Reformed (Calvinist) tradition with them. When the Swedish settlers came, they brought the Swedish Lutheran church to America.

When William Penn colonized Pennsylvania, the "Holy Experiment" was a home for Quakers, or Society of Friends, English and Welsh Baptists, Scottish Presbyterians, and a host of smaller German sects stemming from the Anabaptists in Europe. These German sects included Moravians, Dunkers, Brethren, Schwenkfelders, Mennonites, and German Lutherans. All Protestant Christian groups had in common their European and Reformation origins.

Transferring forms of the Christian faith to the New World gave rise to the strong hope that religious faith and practice would be more pure among adherents. As colonies prospered, and as new settlers arrived and old families moved west to find new land and opportunities, some felt that religious fervor and faith declined. The loss of religion was a favorite theme in sermons in the later 1600s, particularly in New England. Concerned persons sought a spiritual awakening as a way to correct this supposed condition. One form of awakening they pursued was the revival.

REVIVALISM IN THE AMERICAN EXPERIENCE

In the 1730s in New England, a series of "local" awakenings occurred in congregations, primarily in central Massachusetts, with Jonathan Edwards of Northampton as one of the leading revivalists. Simultaneously in New York, New Jersey, and Pennsylvania, similar awakenings began to occur under the leadership of Theodore Frelinghuysen, William Tennant, and his sons Gilbert, John, and William, Jr. Frelinghuysen was Dutch Reformed; the Tennants were Presbyterian. When George Whitefield, a Methodist evangelist from England, toured the colonies from Georgia to Massachusetts in 1739 and 1740, a colony-wide religious revival broke out. This revival is known as the Great Awakening. It affected whole communities and resulted in increased church membership. Many young men became ministers as a result of their spiritual awakening while in college. Generally, the revivals brought positive results, though excesses at some points led to both criticism and opposition.

Nonetheless, the religious revival, or spiritual awakening, became a major phenomenon in American religious life. Other revivals include the Second Great Awakening, or the Great Revival in the West of 1800–1801, the frontier revivals from 1810 to 1830, the urban revivals of the 1860s and 1870s, and the spiritual awakenings of the 1910–1925 and 1949–1958 eras. Thus Americans have witnessed a succession of religious revivals.

These revivals were led by several active evangelists. Charles Grandison Finney took religious revivalism to the cities, including New York City. Dwight L. Moody, a lay preacher, tailored the revival service to city workers' time schedules and used music in new ways. He has been called "the Evangelist to the Machine Age." R. A. Torrey and J. Wilbur Chapman were nationally known

MOODY.

The Evangelist Opens His Meetings.

An Audience of 5000 People at the Pavilion,

And 2000 Disappointed Ones Turned Away.

A headline from the March 11, 1889, issue of the Los Angeles Times.

evangelists at the turn of the century, and Billy Sunday, a Presbyterian and former major league baseball player, filled halls and churches just before and after World War I. In 1949, in Los Angeles, California, a young evangelist announced two weeks of evangelistic meetings in a tent near the downtown area. The two weeks extended to six weeks, and Billy Graham became the most recent of the national-international American evangelists renewing the call for a spiritual awakening.

Some denominations reaped huge benefits from the revival efforts. Those that particularly benefited include the Baptists, the Methodists, the Presbyterians, and later the Holiness churches, such as the Church of the Nazarene, the Free Methodist and Wesleyan Methodist churches, the Pentecostal churches, and most recently the Charismatic movement and some newer, smaller groups.

RELIGION AND THE NEW NATION

Other, quieter forces were at work in America that would directly affect religion. When the Bill of Rights was ratified and the American Constitution became the law of the land, every church body and religious group in the new nation had to live under new conditions. No religion was supported by the state, either nationally or in individual states. Therefore every religious sect, group, or denomination became a voluntary association. This means that the members of the sect, denomination, or group had to fully support their congregation, its buildings, clergy, educational institutions, publishing houses, and, later, national headquarters on a voluntary basis. All religions were also put on an equal footing, with no one favored over any other. These are the principles of separation of church and state, freedom of worship, and religious pluralism—conditions that prevail to this day in American religious life.

The voluntary principle has another meaning in American religious life. Religious leaders and civic leaders could, and did, band together for humanitarian causes. They formed voluntary associations to do missionary work in the United States and overseas. They engaged in promoting literature distribution, educational services, hospital and prison reform, and care of the deaf, the blind, and the insane. These leaders became increasingly concerned for the immigrants and the poor as America's cities began to grow throughout the nineteenth century.

THE AMERICANIZATION OF
THE EUROPEAN CHRISTIAN TRADITION

From the earliest colonial experience, European Christian religious traditions had to be adapted to the new environments in America. With the birth of the nation, these changes were more necessary. And during the nineteenth century in particular, Americanization was a major factor in religious groups and denominations. Immigrants from Europe flooded into America from 1820 to 1920. The Irish built the transportation system, and the Swedes, Norwegians, and Germans filled the cities and rural areas of the midwest. Toward the end of this period the central and southern Europeans—Rumanians, Hungarians, Slavs, Croats, Italians, Polish, Czechs, Spanish, and Portuguese—and European Jews from all countries of Europe formed the work force for an industrializing, urbanizing nation that was bursting at the seams with energy and growing pains. They brought their religious beliefs, customs, and practices with them. Immigrants coming after 1900 established the Eastern Orthodox churches, a group of Christian churches heretofore underrepresented. Various Eastern Orthodox churches and other ethnic churches found a home in the new nation. Many found that their own religious faith was already here, established and settled, but somehow it was not the same as it had been "back home." Whether Lutheran or Roman Catholic or Jewish or in the "Free Church" tradition, old customs and practices had to adapt to new customs and practices in a new land. This process, uneven though it was, is called Americanization. American religious history, in part, is a record of the tensions and turmoil of this process in every religious group with European beginnings—Protestant, Roman Catholic, and Jewish.

"MADE IN AMERICA"

Many denominations and religious sects had only minimal ties to Europe. They really began and flourished within the American experience. The Christian Church–Disciples of Christ grew out of the frontier revivals. The Church of Jesus Christ of Latter-day Saints (the Mormons), the Christian Science Church, the Seventh-Day Adventists, and many of the Holiness-Pentecostal denominations were begun and grew in this nation. These are just a few of the churches or denominations "made in America." Outside the Christian faith, Conservative Judaism took its place alongside Orthodox and Reform Judaism.

MINORITIES IN AMERICAN RELIGION

As America grew, and Americans practiced their religious faith, black people, native Americans, and more recently Spanish-speaking people tended to be neglected or openly treated as less privileged minorities. Black people, slave and free, had to devise their own worship. They adopted the Christian faith but gave it the particular flavor and feeling of the black experience. Black denominations were organized shortly after the American Revolution. The African Methodist Episcopal Church, the African Methodist Episcopal Zion Church, the National Baptist Church, and other predominantly black religious groups have taken their place among American religious groups, but with a significant difference. For black Americans, the church was their only place of freedom to be themselves and the only institution where black people of ability could find a place to serve. For black Americans, the churches were more than a place to worship; they were part of the total black experience in America, central to their whole life and well-being.

Native Americans have fared less well, comparatively. Often the object of missionary effort, American Indians were not encouraged to retain their tribal and family customs, including religious customs. In more recent times, Indian lore, custom, tradition, and religious practice have been more respected by Americans generally.

As for the Hispanics, or Spanish-speaking, they are as different as are the backgrounds from which they came: Cuba, Puerto Rico, Mexico, Spain, South America, and Central America. They live in all parts of the United States. Mostly Roman Catholic in their faith, they are just now seeking more of a voice in their own religious destiny from the churches of the nation, whether as workers in urban centers or as farm or migrant workers.

THE CHURCH IN THE TWENTIETH CENTURY

Many of the "mainline" Protestant churches were divided between the North and South on questions of Negro slavery before the Civil War. Efforts to reunite these divided denominations have been partially successful. Also the conservative elements within these "mainline" churches, sometimes referred to as Fundamentalists or "Evangelicals," became increasingly restive. From about 1910, they began to break away and form their own denominations. These groups are now fully institutional and have their own publishing houses, colleges and seminaries, and missionary outreach programs.

Two major wars and two minor wars directly affected American churches of all faiths. Increasingly, the role of the church in times of war has come to the fore, through church-based peace movements, the status of conscientious objectors, and an increased quest for the meaning of religious faith in such times of crisis. Opposition to the United States' involvement in war reached its height during the Vietnam war, from 1960 to 1972. This opposition, coupled with civil rights marches in the South and racial disturbances in cities in the North, involved some clergy and lay persons in radical activities. The various Christian churches were divided on the questions raised by activists advocating their causes.

New movements and religious groups formed to attempt to capture the mood and concern of the 1960s. Some, such as the Jesus people, were traditionally Christian, even Fundamentalist, in belief. Others, such as the Children of God, were narrow and structured in practice. Some found a new spiritual experience in the Charismatic movement which emphasizes the Baptism of the Holy Spirit and Speaking in Tongues. The Charismatics are in the "mainline" churches and not only in the Pentecostal churches which traditionally have stressed such beliefs. On campuses across America, college groups such as the Campus Crusade for Christ and the Inter-Varsity Christian Fellowship, as well as the Fellowship of Christian Athletes and Young Life in the high schools, have succeeded in drawing large numbers.

Other religious groups, not in the Christian tradition, attracted many followers in the 1960s and into the 1970s. Krishna Consciousness is a form of Hinduism from India, often referred to as devotional Hinduism. The Divine Light Mission attracted followers to the young Maharaj Ji, born in 1957, in another of the Hindu religious traditions of the individual holy man-teacher, or "guru." The Unified Family, followers of a Korean businessman-evangelist Sun Myung Moon, has attracted mainly young people.

Characterized by controversy, it has sent its "Moonies" out to sell flowers, candy, and religious faith. The Black Muslims have flourished among urban blacks in America. Yoga and Zen Buddhism have also gained followings.

And revivalism continues, using the modern technical advantages provided by radio and television. Billy Graham and Oral Roberts are internationally known. Lesser-known "radio preachers" fill the airwaves, proclaiming the Christian faith in its varieties and dimensions.

Born in the ferment of the European Reformation and the challenge of a new, unlimited continent, the church and its adherents crossed the oceans to a new land. Now, almost four hundred years later, the church and its adherents are present throughout the nation—in rural areas, in villages, and in the cities. The ferment continues unabated. In a society devoted to freedom of worship and committed to religious pluralism, it is bound to be that way.

Jesus people at a rally in the United Nations Plaza, New York.

Glossary

Definitions are limited to those that apply to usage of words and phrases within this book. Italic words in the definitions are defined elsewhere in the Glossary.

Abbey. A *monastery* or convent directed by an abbot or abbess, respectively.

Abraham. One of the *patriarchs* of the Old Testament who at God's command led the *Hebrews* out of Mesopotamia toward the Promised Land of Canaan in Palestine (parts of present-day *Israel,* Jordan, and Egypt).

Absolution. Forgiveness for sin given or assured by a *clergy* person (usually after a *confession*).

Afterlife. Life after death.

Almsgiving. Charity; the giving of money, food, or other gifts to the poor, the church, etc.

Anabaptism. A Christian religious movement originating in the sixteenth century in southern Germany and surrounding areas. One of its central *doctrines* was a denial of *infant baptism* and a belief in a "rebirth" in Christ leading to voluntary *baptism.*

Anathema. A solemn condemnation issued by a church authority leading to excommunication.

Angel. A spiritual being especially created by God, having great power and intelligence.

Anglicanism. A general name for the Church of England and related churches. In the United States, Anglicans came to be called Episcopalians.

Anoint. To touch or smear with oil as part of a sacred rite.

Apostles (meaning "to send"). The first twelve *disciples* of Jesus, especially chosen to preach his *gospel.* The original twelve were: Simon (Peter), Andrew, James and John (sons of Zebedee), Matthew, Philip, Bartholomew, Thaddeus, Simon (the Cananaean), James (son of Alphaeus), Thomas, and Judas Iscariot.

Apostolic. Of, relating to, or based on the *apostles.*

Apostolic see. A *diocese* established by an *apostle,* usually referring to the diocese of Rome.

Apostolic succession. The belief that the authority given by Jesus to Peter and other apostles has been handed down in an unbroken line through the generations in the church.

Aramaic. The language spoken by the Jews and other peoples at the time of Jesus.

Archangel. A heavenly being ranking above an *angel.*

Archbishop. The chief *bishop* within a certain church province or district.

Arimathea. A town in ancient Palestine whose location is not known for certain. It was the home of Joseph, one of Jesus' *disciples.*

Atonement. The act of making amends or offering satisfaction to God for having sinned.

Augsburg Confession. A treatise prepared by Philipp Melanchthon in 1530 which sets forth the basic articles of the Lutheran faith. It was presented to a special *council* convened at Augsburg, Bavaria (West Germany).

Augustinian. A member of a religious order whose rule is based on the teachings of St. Augustine of Hippo.

Baptism. The *sacrament* of admission into the membership of the church through the application of or immersion in water along with certain words and signs. Some Christians believe baptism takes away the stain of *Original Sin.*

Baptismal font. The basin or receptacle in a church where the baptismal water is contained and where *baptisms* take place.

Beelzebub. Another name for the devil, or Satan.

Benefit of clergy. The special status given to the *clergy* whereby they could be tried only by *ecclesiastical* courts.

Bethany. A village of ancient Palestine on the *Mount of Olives.*

Bethphage. A village near *Bethany.*

Bethsaida. A town in ancient Palestine on the Sea of Galilee.

Betrothed. Engaged to be married. In former days, the betrothal was a solemn promise or contract for a future marriage and was considered binding on both parties.

Bible. The sacred *Scriptures* of Christianity. It consists of the Old Testament and the *New Testament.*

Bishop. A clergyman who ranks above a *priest* or *minister* and who has the power to ordain new *clergy* and to administer the *sacrament of confirmation.* Typically has administrative functions for a specific area.

Bishopric. The *diocese* of a *bishop.*

Blasphemy. Showing disrespect to God; using sacred objects in an unholy manner.

Burnt offerings. Precious items (animals, for instance) that were sacrificed to God by burning them.

Byzantine Empire. The eastern half of the *Roman Empire* which flourished from the end of the fourth century to the middle of the fifteenth century. Its capital was Constantinople (earlier called Byzantium; present-day Istanbul, Turkey).

Caesar (Augustus, or Octavian). The ruler of the *Roman Empire,* which included Palestine, at the time of Jesus.

Caesarea Philippi. A city of ancient Palestine in the northwest corner of *Galilee.*

Calvinism. A Christian religious movement originating in the sixteenth century in Switzerland; Ulrich Zwingli and John Calvin were its early leaders. One of its historically distinctive *doctrines* was that of *predestination.* Calvinists advocated simplicity of worship and opposed the rich ceremonies and ornamentation of some other churches.

Canonical. In keeping with the code of the church.

Canon law. The code of law followed by the church.

Canossa. A castle in northern Italy where, in the eleventh century, Emperor Henry IV submitted to Pope Gregory VII's power of *investiture*.

Capernaum. A city in ancient Palestine on the Sea of Galilee.

Cardinal. In the Roman Catholic church, the cardinals are the princes of the church and are nominated by the *pope*. They serve as advisors to the pope and elect a new pope upon the pope's death or retirement.

Catechism. A volume (usually in the form of questions and answers) used to instruct candidates in the beliefs and practices of a particular religion.

Cathedral. The main church of a *diocese*, which is the headquarters of a *bishop*.

Catholicism, Roman. A Christian denomination under the spiritual leadership of the *pope*.

Celibacy. Voluntary abstention from sexual relationships and marriage in order to devote oneself to God and his service.

Chief priests. The most influential *priests* among the ancient Jews.

Circumcise. To cut off a person's foreskin, usually for purposes of purification.

Clergy. The group ordained to perform priestly or ministerial duties in the church, as opposed to the *laity*.

Cleric. A member of the *clergy*.

Colossians. Inhabitants of ancient Colossae, a city in what is now west-central Turkey. Also a book in the *New Testament*.

Commandment. One of the ten injunctions given to *Moses* by God, outlining ethical behavior toward God and one's neighbors.

Communion. See *Holy Communion*.

Confession. A statement of religious belief; the recitation of *sins* to God or to a *priest* for the purpose of obtaining forgiveness.

Confessor. One who hears *confessions*, such as a *priest*.

Confirmation. A *sacrament,* or rite, usually administered at the beginning of adolescence, intended to confer the gifts of the *Holy Spirit* and, in some cases, to admit individuals to full church membership.

Congregation. The members of a church assembled for worship or other religious purposes.

Congregational. A form of church government which places all authority in the hands of the local *congregation.*

Consecrated soil. A burial plot that has been blessed by a *priest* or *minister,* implying that the deceased had been a practicing member of a church community.

Consubstantiation. The belief that the bread and wine consumed in *Holy Communion* contain or convey the body and blood of Christ; it does not teach that a change takes place as in *transubstantiation.* Consubstantiation has tended to be a Lutheran teaching as opposed to the Roman Catholic transubstantiation and the Protestant or Reformed teaching that the bread and wine are signs of Christ's body and blood.

Contemplation. Meditation on spiritual matters as a form of devotion.

Conversion. A voluntary "decision for Christ"; an individual religious awakening of *repentance* and faith resulting in a radically changed inner and outer life or attitude. Biblically, the model is the conversion of Saul of Tarsus (St. Paul) on the road to Damascus (Acts 9).

Corinthians. Inhabitants of a city of ancient Greece located in the northern part of the Peloponnesus. Also two books in the *New Testament.*

Council (church). An assembly of church representatives meeting to consider matters of *doctrine,* ritual, discipline, etc.

Council of Chalcedon. A *council* convened in 451 in what is now a part of Istanbul, Turkey. Its purpose was to define *doctrine,* approve statements such as the *Nicene Creed,* and establish disciplinary measures for the *clergy.*

Council of Constance. A *council* convened from 1414 to 1418 in what is now West Germany. It condemned the teachings of John Wycliffe and John Huss and brought about church unity by electing Pope Martin V.

Council of Nicaea. A *council* held in 325 in what is now northwestern Turkey. Not much is known about the council except for its issuance of the *Nicene Creed.*

Council of Trent. A *council* originally convened in 1545 in northern Italy, lasting until 1563. Its most important work was the definition of *doctrine* and the reform of morals and church administration in the aftermath of the *Reformation.*

Covenant. A solemn pledge or promise, such as between God and his people.

Creation. In biblical tradition, God's act of bringing the world and all living things into existence.

Creed. A statement of religious belief, for example, the *Nicene Creed.*

Crucifixion. A Roman form of capital punishment; specifically, the nailing of Jesus to the cross and his subsequent death.

Crusades. The various Christian expeditions during the eleventh, twelfth, and thirteenth centuries whose goal was to wrest the *Holy Land* from the *Muslims.*

Curia (Roman). The governmental body of the Roman Catholic church.

Cyrene. An ancient city in what is now northeastern Libya.

Dalmanutha. City or region near the Sea of Galilee.

David. An Old Testament king who was responsible for unifying the ancient *Hebrews* and building an Israelite kingdom. He was also the author of the biblical songs known as the Psalms.

Deacon (meaning "to serve"). An order of ministry in some churches.

Decapolis. A region of ancient Palestine around the Sea of Galilee.

Denarii. Plural of "denarius," a small coin of ancient Rome.

Diocese. A church territory under the supervision of a *bishop.*

Disciple (meaning "learner" or "student"). Follower of Jesus.

Doctrine. Official teachings of a religious faith.

Dominicans. Members of a religious order founded by St. Dominic in 1215, especially noted for their preaching.

Easter. The feast of the *Resurrection* of Jesus celebrated on various dates in the spring.

Eastern Orthodox. Referring to the various Eastern churches that broke with Rome and that follow a distinctly Eastern rite of worship.

Ecclesiastical. Having reference to a church.

Ecumenical. Relating to church unity or cooperation.

Edict of Milan. A statement issued by Emperor Constantine in 313 granting toleration to all religions in the *Roman Empire.*

Elder. One of the leaders of the *synagogue* in Jesus' time; a church officer or *minister.*

Elect. The special favorites, or chosen, of God.

Elijah. A *prophet* of the Old Testament who brought the Jews back to the worship of the God of *Israel* rather than Baal, an idol.

Ephesians. Inhabitants of the ancient city of Ephesus on the Aegean Sea in what is now western Turkey. Also a book in the *New Testament.*

Episcopal. A form of church government based on *bishops* or overseers.

Epistles. The various letters of the *New Testament,* many of which were written by Paul to groups of Christians he had visited.

Eternal life. Life after death in unity with God.

Eucharist (meaning "thanksgiving"). Refers to the *Holy Communion, Lord's Supper,* or *Mass.*

Evangelism. The more general term used to describe the total attempt of the churches to enlist new members. Particular term used in reference to revivalism.

Evangelism, New. Recent attempt to accommodate the more conservative, or Evangelistic, groups to contemporary mores and life. Not a movement, but young "practitioners" of the Evangelical theological position.

Evangelists (meaning "proclaimers"). Refers to those who actively spread the word of God; Matthew, Mark, Luke, and John—the writers of the *New Testament Gospels.*

Excommunicate. To deny an individual (often a "public" sinner) the rights and privileges of church membership.

Exhorters. Nonordained persons with the ability to "exhort" people, using biblical texts. For some, being an exhorter constituted a first step toward being ordained as a minister. Primarily a Methodist term, though other denominations had exhorters.

Extreme unction. The "last rites" of the church—a *sacrament* of anointing and prayers to comfort the dying.

Fallen asleep (in Christ). Having died in Jesus' good graces.

Fasting. Avoiding food wholly or in part for spiritual discipline.

Feudalism. A system of relationships widespread in *medieval* Europe based on landholding, protection, and mutual obligations between lord and tenant (vassal), overlord and underlord, king and noble, etc.

Fourth Lateran Council. See *Lateran Council, Fourth.*

Franciscans. Members of a religious order founded by St. Francis of Assisi in 1209, especially dedicated to acts of charity.

Free church. Voluntary membership, not supported by the state or government. Also means nonliturgical. Free churches are found in Europe and North America; they are "free," or without dependence on the state or government.

Galilee. The northern region of ancient Palestine where Jesus' home, *Nazareth,* was located.

Gaul. An ancient country comprising areas of present-day France, Belgium, and northern Italy.

Gennesaret, Lake of. Another name for the Sea of Galilee.

Gentiles. Those who are not Jews.

Gerasenes. Inhabitants of the town of Gerasa in ancient Palestine.

Gethsemane. The garden outside Jerusalem where Jesus was betrayed by Judas Iscariot.

Golgotha. A hill outside Jerusalem where Jesus was crucified.

Gospel (meaning "good news"). Refers to the first four books of the *New Testament* written respectively by Matthew, Mark, Luke, and John.

Gothic. Relating to a style of architecture developed in northern France around the middle of the twelfth century and characterized by high vaulted ceilings, pointed arches, and flying buttresses.

Grace. An unearned gift of help from God given to humans to assist in their sanctification.

Hades. The underworld—another term for *hell.*

Heathen. One who does not believe in the God of the *Bible.*

Hebrews. A northern Semitic people to whom the ancient Israelites belonged.

Heidelberg Catechism. A treatise prepared in the 1560s as an attempt to provide an acceptable *confession* of faith for the various *Protestant* churches in the "Reformed tradition." Although the groups were not reconciled, the Catechism is still widely used today.

Hell. A place of everlasting damnation for those who turn against God and die unrepentant.

Helvetic Confession. One of two documents drawn up in Switzerland in the 1560s that state the common beliefs of the Reformed (chiefly Calvinist) churches.

Heresy. Denial of official church *doctrine.*

Herodians. Partisans of the house of Herod the Great, king of *Judea* at the time Jesus was born.

"High" church. Traditionally a designation used for those Anglicans who employ a *liturgy* and other practices similar to that of Roman Catholicism (compare *"Low" church).*

High priest. The head of the ancient Jewish priesthood. Caiaphas was high *priest* at the time of Jesus' *crucifixion.*

Holiness. The following terms are related to what is commonly referred to as Holiness teaching, or Wesleyanism, and to the church bodies who come out of this teaching:

Baptism of the Holy Spirit	Perfect Love
Deeper work of grace	Perfection
Entire sanctification	Sanctification
Filled with the Spirit	Second work of grace
Holiness	Sinless perfection

Holiness teaching disagrees with the premise that when people are converted, or "born again," their *sins* are forgiven and no longer count against them. Rather, Holiness teaching claims that sin itself has not been dealt with or eradicated. Yet by an act of the *Holy Spirit,* an exalted state of "Holiness," or "sinlessness," or "perfection," or "perfect love" can be realized, thus "Baptism of the Holy Spirit." This act of surrender, or being "filled with the Spirit," occurs subsequent to the experience of *conversion,* or the first work of grace, thus "second work of grace." Pentecostals, or Charismatics, believe that the "Baptism of the Holy Spirit" is accompanied by an ecstatic experience called *speaking in tongues,* which is the sign of being filled with the Spirit. This ecstatic experience continues to be central to Pentecostal or Charismatic worship. The biblical source for this experience is Acts 2.

Holy Communion. The *sacrament* in which the body and blood of Jesus Christ in the form of bread and wine are consumed.

Holy Land. A general name for ancient Palestine, where Jesus lived and died.

Holy Sepulcher. The tomb in which Jesus was buried.

Holy Spirit. The third person of the Trinity; the active presence of God in human beings.

Idumea. An ancient country south of *Israel;* also called Edom.

Incarnate, incarnation (meaning "becoming flesh"). Refers to the idea that God took on human form in Jesus Christ.

Index (of forbidden books). A list of books that the Roman Catholic church considers heretical or dangerous to faith or morals.

Infant baptism. Administration of the *sacrament* of *baptism* to one who is not yet mature and thus unable to make a choice.

Inquisition, The. Former Roman Catholic court that sought to uncover and punish *heresy.*

Intercession. A plea or prayer for others.

Interdict. To exclude an entire region or group from the rights and privileges of church membership.

Investiture. The act of naming *bishops* in a particular area or country and giving them the powers and symbols of their office.

Isaac. In the Old Testament, the son of *Abraham* and father of *Jacob.*

Islam. The religion founded by Muhammad in the early seventh century which teaches that there is but one God, Allah, and Muhammad is his *Prophet.*

Israel. An ancient kingdom of Palestine occupied by the *Hebrews.* The present-day republic of Israel was established in 1948.

Jacob. In the Old Testament, the son of *Isaac* who carried on *Abraham's covenant* with God.

Jeremiah. A major *prophet* of the Old Testament.

Jericho. An ancient city of Palestine near the Dead Sea. It was one of the settlements attacked by the Israelites under Joshua as they moved into the Promised Land.

Jesuits. Members of the Society of Jesus, a religious order founded by St. Ignatius of Loyola in 1534, particularly noted for their schools and missions.

Joel. An Old Testament *prophet* and presumed author of the Book (*Prophecy*) of Joel.

Judaism. The religion of the Jews, characterized by a belief in one God.

Judea. The southern region of ancient Palestine.

Justification by faith. A tenet of *Lutheranism* which held that faith alone would lead to salvation.

Justinian's Code. A crucially important reorganization of Roman law commissioned by the *Byzantine* emperor Justinian in the middle of the sixth century.

Kingdom of David. The Old Testament empire established by *David* in ancient Palestine; a symbol to the ancient Jews of an enduring empire.

Kingdom of God. Heaven; the *eternal life* where God reigns supreme.

Laity. The members of the church who are not part of the *clergy*.

Last Judgment. The end of the world, at which time God will make a final judgment to separate the just from the unjust.

Lateran Council, Fourth. A *council* convened in 1215 in Rome. It dealt mainly with *Crusade* matters, *heresy*, the *sacraments* of *penance (confession)* and *Holy Communion*, and church reform.

Legate (papal). An official representative of the *pope*.

Liturgy. The ceremonies, *rites*, practices, and modes of worship prescribed for a religious body.

Lord's Supper, The. *Holy Communion.*

"Low" church. Traditionally a designation used for those Anglicans who enjoy a simpler worship style (compare *"High" church*).

Lutheranism. A Christian religious movement of the sixteenth century led by Martin Luther, one of whose chief tenets was *justification by faith*. Lutheranism was characterized by greater lay participation in worship than was found in Roman *Catholicism* and services in the language of the people. It was particularly influential in northern Europe.

Martyr. One who willingly undergoes death rather than deny his or her religious beliefs.

Mass, The. The central Roman Catholic worship service consisting of introductory rites, proclamation of the Word, and the *sacrament* of *Holy Communion.*

Medieval. Of or pertaining to the *Middle Ages.*

Messiah (meaning "anointed"). One with specific powers and function, sent by God. Christians believe Jesus is the Messiah prophesied in the Hebrew scriptures.

Middle Ages. The period in Europe from about 500 to the start of the *Renaissance,* about 1500.

Minister. One who performs religious functions; in certain *Protestant* denominations, an ordained member of the *clergy.*

Missionaries. *Clergy* or *laity* who go afield to teach others about God.

Mohammed. See *Muhammad.*

Monastery. A house where religious persons, especially monks, live a communal life and perform certain works and devotions in the service of God.

Monasticism. The organized life of work and prayer as practiced in a *monastery.*

Monastic orders. Those religious communities organized around a monastic rule of life, such as the Benedictines.

Monotheism. The belief in one God.

Moses. The great lawgiver of the Old Testament to whom God revealed the Ten *Commandments.*

Moslems. See *Muslims.*

Mount of Olives. A hill east of Jerusalem.

Muhammad (also spelled "Mohammed"). Arab founder of the religion of *Islam,* who lived from 570 to 632 in what is now Saudi Arabia.

Muslims. Followers of the religion of *Islam;* one who submits (to the will of Allah).

Myrrh. A sharp, bitter tree secretion once used in incense and as a perfume.

Nard. A fragrant salve often used in ancient times.

Nazareth. The town in *Galilee* where Jesus lived.

New Testament. The second part of the Christian *Bible,* which deals mainly with the life and teachings of Jesus.

Nicene Creed. The *confession* of faith or belief drawn up at the *Council of Nicaea* in 325.

Ordination. The ceremony that officially grants one priestly or ministerial authority. Regarded by some Christians as a *sacrament.*

Original Sin. The first sin, that of Adam and Eve in the Garden of Eden when they defied God. It also has reference to the hereditary sinfulness of humans since the "Fall of Adam and Eve."

Pagan. A *heathen,* particularly one who worships many gods.

Pantheon. The multiple gods of a group of people such as the ancient Romans.

Papacy. The office of the *pope.*

Papal States. A region in central Italy that was once governed by the *pope.*

Parable. A story that points out a moral or religious principle.

Paradise. The Garden of Eden; heaven, or the place where the soul will be united to God after death.

Parish. An administrative district within a *diocese,* usually headed by a pastor; the area served by a local church; or, in some instances, the local congregation.

Passover. A Jewish feast in spring celebrating the *Hebrews'* freedom from bondage in Egypt.

Patriarch. The head of an *Eastern Orthodox* church; among the ancient *Hebrews,* the head of an important family.

Penance. *Atonement* for sin; a *sacrament* involving *confession* of *sin, repentance,* reconciliation, and absolution or forgiveness in the Roman Catholic church and some other Christian churches.

Penitence. Sorrow for *sin.*

Pentecost (meaning "fiftieth"). A feast on the seventh Sunday (fiftieth day) after *Easter* celebrating the descent of the *Holy Spirit* upon the *apostles.* Generally marks the founding of the Christian church.

Persia. An ancient empire centered in what is present-day Iran.

Petrine Theory. The theory that Christ gave special orders to Peter, and that Peter as first *bishop* of Rome passed this authority to his successors. Has been the basis for the claim to power on the part of the *pope.*

Pharisees. Members of an ancient Jewish sect who believed in a strict observance of the Law of *Moses.*

Phrygia. An ancient country in what is now west-central Turkey.

Pilate, Pontius. The Roman governor of *Judea* at the time of Jesus.

Pilgrim. One who goes on a religious journey, particularly to the *Holy Land.*

Pilgrimage. The journey of a *pilgrim.*

Pontiff. The *pope.*

Pope, The. The *bishop* of Rome, recognized as head of the Roman Catholic church.

Praetorium. The residence of the Roman governor in Jerusalem.

Predestination. The belief that God decrees in advance an individual's ultimate destiny.

Presbyter. In early Christianity and in some Christian denominations today, a member of the church's governing body; an *elder.* May be a minister or priest. *Presbyter* is the root word for the English word *priest.*

Priest. One who has been ordained to perform the *rites* and ministerial duties of a religion—today used mainly in Roman Catholic, Anglican (Episcopal), and *Eastern Orthodox* churches.

Primitive (as in *Primitive Baptist*). A view that opposes missionary outreach, schools and colleges, publishing houses, and special education for the ministry. According to this view, if a person feels "called," he or she is ordained, regardless of training.

Prodigal. Wasteful, referring particularly to Jesus' *parable* about the Prodigal Son.

Prophecy. An inspired foretelling of an event or the act of revealing knowledge or information received from a deity (God).

Prophet. One who is divinely inspired to make *revelations.*

Protestant. Relating to those *Reformation* religious movements and churches that broke away from Roman *Catholicism* and the authority of the *pope* during the sixteenth century.

Purgatory. A state of punishment after death where the soul atones for past *sins* in preparation for entering heaven.

Puritans. Members of an English Calvinist religion who believed in strict, unceremonial worship and life and who attempted to "purify" the Anglican church.

Redemption. Freedom from the effects of *sin,* suffering, and death.

Reformation. The sixteenth-century religious movement that resulted in the breaking away from Roman *Catholicism* and the establishment of *Protestant* churches.

Renaissance. The period in Europe beginning around 1500 (earlier in Italy) and lasting until about the end of the 1700s. It was characterized by a rebirth of interest in ancient Greece and Rome and in the humanities, and an explosion of artistic and literary expression.

Repentance. Sorrow and *atonement* for *sin.*

Restorationism. A term used to refer to one of the basic teachings in the founding of the Christian Church–Disciples of Christ denomination: to "restore" the church in belief and practice to what was taught and practiced by the early Christians as described in the *New Testament,* primarily in the book of Acts.

Resurrection. A rising again to life before the *Last Judgment;* Jesus' return from the dead on *Easter.*

Revelation. Something that is brought to light, particularly a disclosure made by God to human beings.

Revival. A mode of spiritual outreach designed to persuade large groups of people in a relatively short time; a particular kind of *evangelism.*

Revivalist. An *evangelist,* or preacher, who engages in revivalism and emphasizes *sin,* salvation, and *conversion* as an immediate experience. Billy Graham, the best-known contemporary revivalist, adapted revivalism to the "crusade" and to the use of radio and television.

Rite. A prescribed ceremony or ritual.

Roman Catholicism. See *Catholicism, Roman.*

Roman Empire. All the lands and peoples controlled by the emperors of Rome from about 45 B.C. to about A.D. 180. At one time it comprised the entire Mediterranean area, most of Europe and Britain, and sections extending to the Caspian Sea and the Persian Gulf.

Romanesque. Relating to a style of architecture developed in Italy in the eleventh and twelfth centuries. It was based on old Roman models and characterized by rounded arches and thick, massive walls.

Sabbath. The seventh day of the week, one of rest and worship among the Jews.

Sacrament. A "visible sign of an invisible reality." Roman Catholics and *Eastern Orthodox* enumerate seven sacraments: *baptism, confirmation,* marriage, *ordination, Eucharist (Holy Communion), penance,* and *extreme unction.* Most *Protestant* groups emphasize two: baptism and Holy Communion. For all Christians, baptism and Holy Communion have been regarded as the most important sacraments and as those commanded by Christ in the *Gospels.* Some Protestant groups do not observe sacraments but rather the ordinances of baptism and the Lord's Supper.

Sacramental. Of or pertaining to the *sacraments.*

Sacrifice. An offering made to God.

Sacrilege. An indignity against a holy person, place, or object.

Sadducees. Members of an ancient Jewish sect who refused to accept observances not specifically outlined in the Law of *Moses.*

Saint. One especially favored by God, particularly when officially declared so by the church; one made holy by God's grace.

Samaria. A district of ancient Palestine south of *Galilee.*

Savior. Jesus Christ in his role as rescuer from *sin.*

Scribes. Members of the learned class of the ancient Jews; specialists in the *Scripture.*

Scriptures. The Old and *New Testaments;* the sacred writings of a religion.

See. A *diocese.*

Separatists. Those who chose to leave the Anglican church rather than try to reform it.

Shema, The. The Jewish *confession* of faith. Found in Deuteronomy 6:4–9: "Hear, O Israel: the Lord Our God, the Lord is One."

Sidon. One of the principal cities of ancient Phoenicia, in what is now Lebanon.

Sign of the cross. A hand gesture made on oneself or toward others as a blessing.

Sin. An offense against God.

Son of Man. Jesus Christ.

Speaking in tongues. Being able to speak so as to be understood by people of different nationalities; ecstatic speech during a highly emotional religious experience.

Stake. A post to which a person is tied for execution; an administrative area within the Mormon church system.

Syllabus. An outline of a formal treatise or paper.

Synagogue. A Jewish house of worship.

Synod. A church *council.*

Temple (of Jerusalem). The place of worship for the Jews of the city.

Tenet. A *doctrine* or belief.

Theology. The systematic study of God and his relations with humanity.

Thessalonians. Inhabitants of an ancient city that is now Salonika, in northern Greece. Also two books in the *New Testament.*

Tithes. Revenue paid to a church, representing ten percent of one's income.

Transfigured. Changed in form and appearance.

Transubstantiation. The *doctrine* that the consecrated bread and wine truly become the body and blood of Jesus Christ in the act of consecration.

Trinitarian. Of or relating to the Holy Trinity (the *doctrine* of the unity of the Father, the Son, and the *Holy Spirit*).

Twelve, The. See *Apostles.*

Tyre. One of the principal cities of ancient Phoenicia, in what is now Lebanon.

Usury. Charging interest (today, excessive interest) on money loans.

Vestments. The ceremonial clothing and symbols worn by *clergy* or church officiants in services and ceremonies.

Virgin birth. The *doctrine* that Mary gave birth to Jesus through the power of the *Holy Spirit* and without human intercourse.

Westminster Confession. A statement of Calvinistic *doctrine* drawn up in England in 1648 and serving as a standard for many English-speaking Presbyterian churches.

Worldliness. A concern with and preference for this world as opposed to the other world—heaven.